Table of Contents

No. 102.)   (May, 1880.

GIGANTIC SUPPLEMENTS,
YOUNG LADIES' JOURNAL.

Victorian Fashions Volume I 1880-1890

by Hazel Ulseth & Helen Shannon

Edited by Donna H. Felger

Photography by Hazel and Marty Ulseth.

Published By

HOBBY HOUSE PRESS, INC.
Cumberland, Maryland 21502

Dedication

To Pat Stall in recognition of her love of dolls, her creativity and her generous contributions which have added so much to the world of doll collectors.

Additional Copies of this book may be purchased at $14.95
from
HOBBY HOUSE PRESS, INC.
900 Frederick Street
Cumberland, Maryland 21502
or from your favorite bookstore or dealer.
Please add $2.50 per copy postage.

ISBN: 0-87588-309-5

Nov.75

Hist. Pres. Grant

Nov. 1996

DER BAZAR, BERLIN, November 1, 1881.

DER BAZAR, BERLIN, July 1, 1882.

DER BAZAR, BERLIN, August 1, 1882.

DER BAZAR, BERLIN, February 1, 1883.

LA MODE ILLUSTRÉE, PARIS, 1884.

JOURNAL DES DEMOISELLES, PARIS, 1887.

FRONT VIEW

Our pattern is shown for this delightful doll at the back of this book. She is costumed in a silk dress adapted from *Delineator*, May 1890, which features a bouffant skirt with wide lace trim topped by a unique bodice tapered to a point at center front. A triangular inset of lace is bordered by an overlay at each side, and large ribbon bows at each shoulder.

A mandarin collar finishes the neckline. Full sleeves end with lace-covered cuffs. Completing our doll's party outfit, this charming velvet cloak shows fullness slightly gathered on a simple yoke, with bands of blonde mink edging center fronts and yoke edge. The same trim is featured on a simple cap bonnet. Her muff is mink with a silk lining. The doll shown here is a 23½in (60cm) Jumeau.

BACK VIEW

LEFT: 23½in (60cm) Jumeau marked: "DÉPOSÉ//Tête Jumeau//Bte SGDG//11 H."; human hair wig, paperweight eyes, molded ears, closed mouth, ball-jointed body. Body is marked: "Jumeau Medaille D'or//Paris."

RIGHT: 23in (59cm) Jumeau marked in red stamp: "DEPOSE//TETE JUMEAU//Bte SGDG//11." Paperweight eyes, closed mouth, ball-jointed body.

1881
Misses' Dress

No. 8252. — Plain and striped dress goods are united in the construction in the present instance, and while the plain fabric is visible only in under-facings, it serves in a very tasteful manner to develop a contrast. The dress is shaped in Princess fashion with a bust dart and an underarm dart in each side of the front and side-back seams and curved closing edges at the back. The closing is made only to a little below the waistline, and the side-back seams terminate in a line with it, the fullness at the extremities being folded underneath to form two box-plaits on the outside. The closing edges are faced, and buttonholes and medium-sized carved pearl buttons are employed in performing the closing. Upon the bottom of the front and sides of the dress is a narrow ruffle of the material, gathered and set on to form its own heading and edged at both sides with lace. Upon the back are three ruffles similar to this, save that they are edged only at the bottom with lace and are each over-lapped slightly at their upper edge by the one next in succession. These three ruffles are sur-mounted by another, finished and set on in the same manner as that on the front. Upon each side is a unique and pretty drapery which is in the form of a deep, irregularly-shaped gore, under-faced at its lower and front edges with plain goods and laid in four upward-turning plaits at its back edge. The back edge is inserted in the underarm seam with the top a becoming distance below the waistline, the upper edge being first sewed to position and the drapery then turned over to conceal the seam. The upper front corners meet at the center of the front, and then the draperies flare as far as their broadest portions, where they are again caught together, their edges flaring again below this for the remainder of their length. This arrangement causes each drapery to fall over in a loop or loose plait and exposes the under-facing prettily. Plaited ribbons are inserted in the underarm seams at the tops of the draperies, and their ends are tied in a large sash bow across the back. The sleeves are in coat shape, and each is finished at the wrist with a lace-trimmed ruffle set on to form its own heading. There is a standing collar about the neck, and outside of this is adjusted a sailor collar, which has a bias under-facing about the upper edge and is bordered at all its outer edges with lace.

Dresses of this style are pretty and fashionable for home, school and street wear. The mode is adapted to the simplest textures in vogue, as well as to the airy and dressy materials selected for dancing-school and juvenile parties. A pretty dress for

8252
Front View.

8252
Back View.

general wear is of claret-colored cashmere, with draperies of striped claret-and-gold Surah, and bows of the latter material. The sailor collar is also of the striped goods and the sleeve and skirt trimmings are the same as in the present instance. The method of construction affords opportunity for the development of any tasteful combination, and is also adapted to the use of one kind of material throughout, though uniformity is not so desirable.

Pattern No. 8252 is appropriate for misses from eight fo fifteen years of age.

1881
Girls' Costume

No. 8188. — A dainty and comfortable little costume is here exhibited. The top is a deep, square yoke, to which the body-portion is joined at each side of the arms'-eyes. The body has three box-plaits in the front and three at the back, the plaits being stitched to position a little below the waistline and then permitted to fall loosely in their folds, so as to impart the requisite fullness to the skirt. The back is closed with buttonholes and buttons to a little below the waistline, and below this the closing is permanent and invisible. The material used in the costume is sheer zephyr gingham, and three encircling rows of braid provide a garniture for the lower part of the plaited body. Ruffles of the material, finished to form self-headings, trim the neck and the wrists of the sleeves, the latter being in easy coat style.

Oftentimes, the yoke and sleeves of dresses of this style will be in decided contrast with the body; lace or embroidered net, or strips of lace, or of Swiss French or Hamburg insertion being the prettiest on Summer dresses, whether the body be of a silk, woolen or cotton fabric. Lovely little dresses, with yokes and sleeves of embroidered net, have the bodies of fine cashmere, finished at the bottom with wide hems herring-boned to position with silk floss. A row of herring-bone stitching may also be made down the center of cash-plait, with very pretty results. Cambrics, ginghams, lawns, cashmeres, nuns'-cloth, Surahs, Summer silks, pongees, foulards, are all stylish for such dresses, with white embroidery or for the yokes and sleeves.

No. 8233. — The popularity of the kilt is as great this season as ever before, and certainly a more pleasing bit of information than this could not be conveyed by the pen of Fashion, for it is one of the most healthful, as well as most becoming, styles of skirt ever introduced for the little folks. The present illustrations show a costume of light cloth, having a kilt skirt attached to an under-waist and an outside body in jacket form. The skirt is formed of straight breadths, joined together to obtain the requisite width and turned under for a hem at the lower edge. The top is laid in kilt-plaits turning from the center of the front, and these plaits, after being pressed, are held in position by means of a tape sewed to them on the under side about half-way between the top and bottom. A placket-opening is cut beneath the fold of the plait at the center of the back, and the skirt is then ready to be attached to the waist. The latter portion, not being visible when the jacket is adjusted, is made of Silesia. It is loosely fitted by seams upon the

Figure No. 5 — GIRLS' COSTUME.

shoulders and under the arms, and the edges of the closing are curved to aid in the process and are under-faced with the material to prepare them for the buttonholes and flat buttons used in closing. The neck is low enough to be invisible above the jacket, and both it and the arms-eyes are finished with narrow bindings. The waist extends well below the hips and permits the skirt to hang easily and gracefully, without the slightest possibility of disarrangement.

The jacket is double-breasted from the throat to a little below the waistline, and the buttonholes are worked in a fly sewed beneath the overlapping side. But one row of buttons is used in closing the garment, and this is, of course, invisible, owing to the fly. Below the closing the two sides slant off toward the back with a considerable flare, which gives a jaunty diagonal effect to the front. In each side is an underarm dart, which, with the seams upon the shoulders and at the sides and a curving seam down the

center, fits the garment in the most becoming manner. The side seams terminate a short distance below the waistline, and the adjoining corners of the back are turned over on the outside in triangular *revers* that are faced with plush; and across the back, between the corners of the *revers*, is fastened a frog of silk cord. A wide band of plush borders the closing and lower edges of the fronts, and upon each side, where an opening for a pocket would naturally be cut, a frog of cord is arranged in curved outline. Very often an opening will be cut in one or both sides between the double lines of braid and pockets will be inserted. The sleeve is in coat shape, and is prettily ornamented at the wrist with a pointed cuff-facing of plush. A rolling collar of plush encircles the neck and completes the accessories of the garment.

Girls from three to nine years of age will find this costume an attractive addition to their wardrobe.

8233
Front View.

8233
Back View.

8188
Front View.

8188
Back View.

MISSES' COSTUME.

1882
Misses' Costume

A dressy costume of plain and striped Summer silk is here delineated. The skirt is of the striped silk and is plainly finished at the bottom. It is of the fashionable four-gored shape, and is over-draped in a quaint and novel manner. The draperies are all of plain silk. The back-drapery forms a *bouffante* point, plaited up prettily at one side and undraped at the other. The front-drapery comprises two sections plaited up at their front edges, where they are seamed together, the seam coming low down upon the center of the front-gore. Above this seam the edges flare widely so as to expose the striped silk of the skirt, the flaring edges being sewed flatly to position and ornamented with turn-back frills of lace, the frill on the right-drapery being carried down over the seamed plaited edges and also about the lower edge of the same drapery. The lower edge of the left drapery is trimmed to correspond, as are also all the edges of the back-drapery. The skirt pattern is appropriate for misses from eight to fifteen years of age.

The waist is plain and round, with a belt at its lower edge, and is closely fitted by nicely graded darts and seams. It has a deep, square Pompadour simulated upon the front with lengthwise strips of insertion and a border frill of lace, and about the neck is a double ruche of lace. The sleeves are prettily fashioned, and are each ornamented at the wrist with a double frill of lace and a band and bow of pretty ribbon. When the belt and skirt are adjusted, a wide sash of ribbon is folded about the waist and tied in front in a careless bow with long, floating ends.

1882
Girls' Costume

No. 8198. — This engraving exhibits one of the most beautiful of this season's modes in costumes for the little lady. The material is cream-white cashmere and the sash is of the material with realistic-looking roses embedded in their foliage embroidered upon it so as to appear as if they were carelessly sprinkled over the surface. The body is clinging and imparts a slender appearance to the figure of the little wearer. It closes at the back with buttonholes and buttons and is lengthened into costume depth by a skirt laid in uniform box-plaits all around. The plaits are made close together and upon the lower part of each is a lengthwise row of three buttons. A deep hem finishes the bottom of the skirt, and the sash is draped gracefully over the joining seams and tied in a large, *négligé* bow at the back. A row of very narrow embroidery edges the wrists of the sleeves, which are further adorned by fancy cuffs simulated with a row of insertion and a frill of deep embroidery. A standing row of narrow embroidery and a falling row of wide embroidery are seamed together to form a pretty ruche for the neck.

The pattern to this handsome little costume is in seven sizes for girls from three

GIRLS' COSTUME.

8198
Front View.

8198
Back View.

to nine years of age. Its simple construction renders it an admirable mode for the various Summer fabrics in vogue for girls' costumes, and while the costume may be quite elaborately garnitured, yet it is so ornamental in itself that no decoration at all need be used and the result will still be stylish and pretty. Laces, embroideries, flat bands, braids, etc., are all fashionable trimmings for it. The sash may be of ribbon or any preferred contrasting fabric, but the prevailing fancy is now for sashes of the costume goods.

1882
Girls' Costume

No. 8202. — Neatness and simplicity are attractive features of the bewitching little costume here pictured. The material is plain Summer silk and a small quantity of embroidered silk of a contrasting color is introduced in the trimming. The front clings easily to the form without the aid of darts and the back has nicely curved back edges, which are underfaced with the material and closed with hooks and loops. The body extends far over the hips to produce a gracefully slender effect and a full skirt is gathered to its lower edge, lengthening it ornamentally to the required depth a costume. A wide band of embroidered silk borders the lower edge of the skirt; a narrower band covers the seam joining the skirt and body. A band of embroidered silk is also arranged down the back at each side of the closing, terminating under the top of the one about the lower part of the body. A similar band heads the tiny ruffles of silk at the wrist of the coat sleeve. The standing collar is of embroidered silk and completes the ornamental items of the costume.

Lace and embroidery are the most fashionable trimmings for such costumes but where variety in the little woman's

GIRLS' COSTUME.

8202
Front View.

8202
Back View.

wardrobe is desired, bands, braids, ruffles and tiny plaitings will afford a pretty deviation. All sorts of materials including ginghams, lawns, percales, muslins, prints and so forth make up into lovely little costumes of this style and only the simplest decoration need to be added. A sash may be worn if a dressy effect be desired.

1882
Girls' Costume

No. 8231. — There is an air of complete-ness and adaptability for street as well as for house wear about the costume, that will make it particularly popular for the pretty fabrics that have come in for Autumn wear. Lady's-cloth of a soft and not too heavy quality is represented in the present instance, and a sash of soft Surah silk is the only extraneous garniture. The fronts are turned under in wide hems and united with button-holes and buttons, and in each side is an underarm dart, which removes all unneces-sary fullness, without rendering the adjust-ment too close. The body portion of the back has center and side-back seams, and reaches only far enough below the waistline to give the fashionable long-waisted effect, the deficiency in depth being made up by a skirt, which is laid in double box-plaits at the top and sewed to the lower edge, its side edges being sewed to the corresponding edges of the fronts. The bottom of the skirt and the lower edges of the fronts are turned under for hems; the plaits are held in their folds by being well pressed. There are two sections comprised in the formation of the sash, the length and width necessary to a proper effect being accurately given in the pattern. One end of each section is straight and the other is bias and is laid in two upturning plaits. The plaited ends are then sewed together and also sewed through this seam over the center seam of the back, extendng for a short distance upon the skirt. Two short straps, each of which is pointed at one end, are sewed upon each side of the costume, the forward one being placed so that its back edge is about even with the underarm dart, while the other is over the side-back seam. These straps are sewed to position at their straight edges and then turned up and caught at the points. The sash ends are then slipped under the straps and tied in front in a pretty bow. A button ornaments each strap near the point, and apparently holds it in position. The sleeves are in coat shape and are each finished with a narrow strap of the material, one end of which is inserted in the outside seam while the other end is pointed and ornamented with a button on the upper side of the sleeve. The neck is bound with a bias strip of silk and outside of it is arranged an ornamental collar laid in small box-plaits. This ornament is stitched to position about an inch from the top, the narrower portion forming a close ruche about the neck, while the deeper part flares just enough to sit easily.

This costume is for girls three to nine years of age.

GIRLS' COSTUME.

8231
Front View.

8231
Back View.

1882
Girls' Costume

No. 8217. — The construction of this little costume is so simple that many mothers will make more than one like it for their little daughters. The front is cut on a fold of the goods, and the adjustment is performed by seams upon the shoulders and under the arms and nicely arched side-back seams reaching to the arms'-eyes. The back edges are curved and under-faced to within a few inches of the bottom, and are seamed together for the remainder of their length. Upon each side of the front, far enough below the waistline to give the fashionable long-waisted effect, is a little *panier* drapery, which is gathered twice at its upper edge and sewed flatly to position through the shirrings. The back edge is diagonal for a part of its length; this portion is sewed flatly upon the dress nearly to the top of the straight portion, which is shirred up in *panier* fashion and inserted in the side-back seam. The front corners of the drapery meet at the center of the front, and the rounding edges are finished with two rows of machine-stitching — a very popular completion for the material represented in the present instance, which is flannel. Ribbons are fastened at the back ends of the shirrings in

8217
Front View.

8217
Back View.

the top and tied in a pretty bow over the front corners, and wider ribbons are plaited over the shirred edges of the *paniers* and arranged in a sash-bow at the termination of the closing. There is a narrow box-plaiting upon the bottom of the costume, and still narrower plaitings finish the wrists of the little coat sleeves. A standing collar with rounding front ends is about the neck, and some distance below this is a collar-like

ornament, the deepest portions of which fall over the tops of the sleeves and are deeply notched, a smaller notch being cut from the center of the front and the ends clipped off at the back to correspond. The edges of this ornament are finished with machine-stitching.

This pattern is appropriate for girls three to nine years of age.

1882
Girls' Costume

No. 8216. — Simplicity is a characteristic feature of this costume but there is a grace and variety about it that is particularly pleasing and yet is really due to its very simplicity. The body portion is long-waisted and shapely, but involves only a few seams in its adjustment, having, in addition to those upon the shoulders and under the arms, only side-back seams extending to the arms'-eyes. The closing edges are curved to assist in the process, and are finished with under-facings. Buttons and buttonholes are used in closing them and below the closing each center-back section falls in a sharp point, producing a sort of basque effect. The skirt is formed of short, straight breadths, joined together to obtain the requisite dimensions. The lower edge is turned under for a hem and the top is gathered and sewed to the body portion as far as the side-back seams, being joined between these to a band that passes under them. The seam joining the skirt to the body is concealed by a shirred, girdle-like strip, which is cut crosswise, turned under at each end about an inch as if for a hem, and shirred twice in front of each under-folded edge. Three shirrings are made through the center, and the girdle is adjusted

8216
Front View.

8216
Back View.

upon the costume with its lower edge just over the seam and is sewed to position through all the shirrings. The ends of the girdle extend only to the side-back seams and, therefore, do not detract from the pointed outline of the back, but rather serve to emphasize its effectiveness. Checked gingham is the material represented in the present instance, and at the wrists of the coat-shaped sleeves are gathered ruffles of the same set on to form their own heading. The neck of the dress is bound with a bias strip, which is, however, concealed by a gathered ruffle similar to those on the sleeves. Buttonholes and medium-sized pearl buttons are used in closing.

Either cotton or woolen suit goods make up prettily in this way. Sometimes the entire skirt will be formed of a deep flounce of embroidery, or it will be plain and be overlaid with ruffles of lace or embroidery. A pretty costume of pearl gray cashmere has the skirt trimmed with ruffles of the same and Saxon embroidery, the embroidery being worked on cashmere of the same shade. The frills at the neck and wrists are of embroidery, and the girdle consists of two strips of embroidery joined together and wrinkled so as not to show the seam.

This is a desirable costume for girls from three to nine years of age.

1882
Child's Costume

No. 8235. — While exceedingly simple, the costume is very effective and forms a very becoming mode for little folks of either sex. The costume comprises a kilt skirt with a plain body and an outside jacket, and in the present instance is represented as made of cashmere, with ribbon ties and fancy metal buttons for garnitures. The skirt is formed of straight breadths, joined together and turned under for a hem at the lower edge. A plait, turning backward, is laid at each side of the center, giving the effect of a wide box-plait at the center upon the outside; all the remaining plaits are laid closely together and turn backward. They are well pressed in their fold and about half-way between the top and bottom they are tacked with a strong thread beyond the possibility of disarrangement.

The body or waist portion is very simple in construction, and serves principally to uphold the skirt. It is fitted by seams upon the shoulders and under the arms, and its back edges are turned under for hems and closed with buttonholes and flat buttons. The neck is sufficiently low to be invisible above the jacket, and is finished with a narrow binding; the arms'-eyes have narrow bias under-facings sewed to them. Before the skirt is added, the hems are lapped flatly at their lower corners and sewed together: after the skirt and waist have been joined, broad ribbon ties, each laid in plaits at one end, are fastened at the extremities of the underarm seams. The free ends are then brought to the center of the front and tied in a handsome bow.

The jacket possesses many of the features of the favorite cutaway style. The fronts meet at the throat and then slant off diagonally toward the bottom with considerable of a flare, the two sides falling apart sufficiently to disclose the arrangement of the sash upon the front. There is an underarm dart in each side, which, with curving side seams and a center seam, adjusts the garment with sufficient closeness to the figure. The center seam is discontinued a little below the waistline, and upon the edges below its termination are cut extensions, which are lapped from the left side over the right and tacked to position at the top, the overlapping edge being ornamented with a row of small buttons and simulated buttonholes set closely together. Upon each side rests a long and not very wide pocket, which is slanted off diagonally at its back edge and decorated at the top with a row of buttons and buttonholes matching those on the back, the buttonholes being above the buttons. The sleeve is in coat shape, and its only decora-

8235
Front View.

8235
Back View.

8230
Front View.

8230
Back View.

CHILD'S COSTUME

CHILD'S COSTUME

tions are four buttons and simulated buttonholes arranged in a line upon the upper side in front of the outside seam. A hook and loop are used in closing the fronts at the throat, and a tasteful item is added to the decorations by arranging buttons down the right side and working or simulating buttonholes upon the left side. A round, flat collar with a seam at the center lends a pretty finish to the neck.

No. 8230. — White lawn is the material used in the construction of this dainty costume. The little skirt is four-gored, and is attached to a belt at the top. It is trimmed about the lower edge with a ruffle of deep embroidery and above this with three ruffles of narrower embroidery, the trimming almost entirely concealing the skirt. The little over-dress has a pointed vest, which is coquettishly displayed between the nicely curved edges of the cutaway fronts and is closed all the way down with buttonholes and tiny pearl buttons. The back is made to cling gracefully by the use of a nicely curved center seam and low side-back gores, and falls in two deep points, the fronts descending in points in a similar manner over the hips.

All the points are prettily wrinkled by upward-turning plaits fastened at the side and center seams beneath dainty little bows of bright ribbon. All the edges of the over-dress are bordered with a row of the narrow embroidery, set on, except at the vest edges, under a tiny band of the material. A narrow band finishes the neck, and a collar, made of embroidered ruffles and insertion, is tied about the neck with ribbons. The dainty little sleeves are tastefully trimmed with a ruffle of embroidery headed by a band of the material.

Woolen, silk and cotton textures of all varieties are charming for such little costumes, and lace and embroidery will be the most fashionable and dressy garnitures. For a little party dress, the mode is especially pretty and may be as elaborately decorated as the maker may desire. When woolen or silk fabrics are used for costumes of this description, the vest may contrast either in texture or in color, or in both, with the skirt and over-dress.

Pattern No. 8230 is appropriate for children from two to six years of age.

1883
Ladies' Toilette

Skirt No. 8661 — Basque No. 8662. The toilette here depicted illustrates a superb mode for gala and afternoon and evening costumes during the coming season. The material is delicate pink nun's-vailing. The skirt is fashioned in the four-gored style, and upon its front-gore is a box-plaited panel which extends from the foot nearly to the belt. The side-gores are decorated with a deep flounce-trimming plaited to correspond with the panel, and upon the lower part of every box-plait are embroidered artistically grouped daisies and buds in their natural tintings of white and gold, with olive for the stems and foliage. The effect is very rich and beautiful, as well as decidedly novel. The front-drapery is all in one to a little below the belt, and below this point is shaped to fall with somewhat of a plain panel effect upon the sides, the front edges flaring widely to expose the box-plaited panel upon the front-gore. Two upward-turning plaits in each back edge relieve the drapery from the severe effect of straight panels, crosswrinkling them slightly but gracefully. The back-drapery is long, and is rendered *bouffant* by deep, downward-turning plaits in its side edges and clustered plaits tacked to the skirt at the center. Three rows of pink satin ribbon about an inch wide border the edges of the front and back draperies, making a handsome and simple garniture. Nun's-vailings in all shades will be especially charming made up in this way; but cashmeres, lawns, sateens, pongees, Summer silks and thin and thick textures of all kinds are equally appropriate. The back-breadth and side-gores may be trimmed alike, if desired; ruffles of the material or of lace or embroidery, plaitings, ruches, etc., being equally stylish garnitures. Flat trimmings will be most effective on the drapery edges, whether they be of lace, ribbon, embroidery or braid.

The basque is superb in design and its elegant fitting is secured by double bust darts, underarm and side-back gores and a center seam, all beautifully curved. It is pointed at the center of the front and arched effectively over the hips; its center and side-back portions fall in long, pointed tabs, which are decorated with embroidered daisies to correspond with the floral adornments on the skirt. Three rows of satin ribbon border the lower edges of the sides and front, and the result is very beautiful. Daisies, intertwined in vine pattern with their buds and sparse foliage, are embroidered upon the front at each side of the closing and extend in artistic fashion across the shoulders nearly to the center seam of

LADIES' TOILETTE

the back. Similar designs decorate the wrists of the sleeves, and the work and the blending of the colors are so well done that a strikingly realistic effect is produced. A standing collar, and a lace ruff forming a *jabot* at the throat, complete the neck. It is an exquisite fashion for all varieties of dress goods, whether cotton, silk or woolen, and may be simply completed or fully-decorated, as most in harmony with the skirt garnitures.

1883 Costume

No. 8659. — Cashmere of a dainty shrimp-pink shade composes this exceedingly stylish costume and Irish point embroidery forms the decoration on the body and front-drapery. The graceful fitting of the deep, round basque-front of the costume is due to single bust and underarm darts; and to the lower edge of the front are joined front and side skirt-gores, which complete the costume depth suitably. The back is superbly fitted by center and side-back portions, which are so planned that the entire back-drapery is provided by the center portions and the entire back skirt by the side-back portions. A broad, double box-plait formed in the top of the back skirt, and another folded underneath at the end of the center seam, throw sufficient ampleness into the drapery and back skirt; and the *bouffant* appearance of the back-drapery is attained by ingenious loopings and tackings at the center and side edges. The front-drapery is prettily cross-plaited, and is shaped at the top to join the front in the becoming curves of a pointed bodice. It has a border-frill of wide Irish point at the lower edge, from beneath which descends a kilted drapery that is blind-hemmed at the lower edge and has all its plaits turning from the center of the front. This kilted drapery falls over the top of a flounce, that is kilt-plaited in the same manner and extends entirely about the foot of the costume. Buttons and buttonholes close the front, and to the overlapping side a frill of embroidery is sewed to turn backward from the buttons, thus permitting the closing to be made without detriment to the embroidery. A standing collar is about the neck, and a *crêpe lisse* ruff and a cravat bow of satin ribbon supply the *lingerie*. The coat sleeves are slightly shortened, and the lower edge of each is bordered with two frills of embroidery below a deep upturned row.

Combinations of two or more materials are especially effective in costumes of this style; the pretty plain and flowered sateens and foulards being exceedingly handsome. For cashmeres, clothes, flannels, checked and Summer silks, pongees, nun's-vailings and dress textures of all kinds either alone or in combination, the mode is both dressy and stylish. Lace or embroidery may decorate such costumes, but a simple finish is also pretty and will usually be adopted when the texture is cloth or similar goods. The deep plaiting is provided for in the pattern, but may be omitted if an elaborate garniture of lace or embroidery be preferred. The foot trimming may be little plaitings or ruffles or a full ruche with handsome results.

LADIES' COSTUME

8659
Front View.

8659
Side-Back View.

1883 Ladies' Costume

No. 8657. — This costume is also illustrated in a combination of plain and floriated sateen, with plain material and embroidery for trimming, at Ladies' figure No. 4.

The popularity of sateens, buntings and other textures of moderate price calls for more variations in the styles of costumes than ever before, because the furor for these tasteful fabrics makes it possible to construct a greater number of toilettes without adding to the expense of a Summer wardrobe. Cream-colored bunting is the material chosen for illustration in the costume pictured in these engravings, and ruffles of the same and lace constitute the garnitures. The skirt is of the fashionable walking shape, and consists of three gores for the front and sides and a full breadth for the back. The gores are fitted to the hips by darts, and the breadth is opened through the center for some distance from the belt for a placket, the fullness at each side of the opening being reduced to the proper size by gathers. A belt is sewed to the top, and tapes are fastened under the side-back seams to tie the fullness in position. Three gathered ruffles, each about seven inches deep when finished, trim the skirt very stylishly; each of the lower ruffles being bordered with lace at its lower edge, and the topmost one, which is set on to form its own heading, at both edges.

The over-dress is a very effective polonaise. It is quite short in front and is closed with buttonholes and buttons. It is cut high in the neck, although the engraving shows a Pompadour shape, which is obtained by cutting the neck out at perforations marked in the pattern. The right side is turned under for a hem and the left is under-faced, and below the closing each side is rounded off in *panier* fashion toward the back, two shallow, upturning plaits being laid in each back edge. Double bust darts, underarm darts, side-back seams and a center seam perform the adjustment in the most elegant manner possible. The side-back seams terminate a little below the waist-line, and the fullness at the end of each is folded in a wide, backward-turning plait underneath, the edges of the plait at the top being run together and the corners tacked one upon the other. Each half of the back is deepened in a long, tapering point below the seam joining it to its respective portion of the front, and these points are raised in a particularly graceful fashion by means of a lengthwise row of shirring made through the center seam from its lower extremity to a point in a line with the terminations of the side-back seams.

8657
Front View, showing the Neck cut out in Pompadour style.

8657
Side-Back View, showing a High Neck, with Military Collar.

Figure No. 4. — LADIES' TOILETTE.

When this shirring is drawn up, the center back drapery is quite short and the points fall together in stylish folds. The shirring, itself, is concealed by an ornamental strap of the goods which is pointed at one end and straight at the other. The straight end is fastened underneath the top of the shirring, and the pointed end is brought upward upon the outside and fastened over the center seam a little above the top of the shirring. This arrangement gives the drapery the appearance of being upheld by the strap and imparts a pleasing carelessness of effect,

which the initiated are very apt to discover, however, to be the result of careful effort. The sleeves are beautifully fitted to the arms and are cut to extend to the wrists, though in this instance they are shortened to a little below the elbow and finished with standing and falling frills of lace. A standing collar for the neck is included in the pattern; but, when the Pompadour neck is preferred, the collar will be omitted; a ruching, formed of a standing and a falling frill of lace, taking its place and finishing the edges of the Pompadour.

1883 Misses' Outdoor Costume

No. 8644. — This charming costume is made of plain foulard silk, for which texture, as well as for white and colored wash goods, and also for sateens, mulls, nun's-vailings and soft, pretty fabrics of all kinds, it is an elegant and stylish fashion. The skirt is of the four-gored shape and is ornamented with a deep flounce of the material reaching nearly half-way to the belt. The flounce is shirred to form a ruffled heading above three small puffs; its lower edge is invisibly hemmed.

The over-dress has a short, pointed bodice front, fitted by single bust darts and narrow underarm gores. It closes in front with buttonholes and buttons, and to the lower edge of the front at each side is gathered a short, found *panier*, which is plaited at its back edge. The *paniers* just meet at the end of the closing and their lower edges are trimmed with a frill of Irish point embroidery. The back of the over-dress is in polonaise fashion, with nicely curved center and side-back seams. These seams terminate in extra widths a little below the waistline, the widths at the side-back seams being disposed in backward-turning plaits underneath, while that at the center seam is shirred through the center for several inches below the top. The shirring is drawn up closely and fastened over the lower part of the seam, causing the fullness at each side to form a handsome sash loop. Two over-lapping plaits in each side edge finish the draping of the back, the result obtained by this simple means being a *bouffant* drapery somewhat shorter at the center than at the sides. Embroidery borders the edges of the back-drapery, with charming effect. The sleeves are of coat shape, extending to the wrist, where they are neatly finished with an upturned row of embroidery. A military collar encircles the neck, which is simply completed by a linen choker-collar and a cravat bow of ribbon. Any other style of *lingerie* preferred may, however, be adopted, deep lace collars being youthful and pretty.

Deep puffs of the material and ruffles or plaiting of the same or of lace or embroidery are fashionable skirt garnitures for such costumes, and are especially beautiful and effective when light textures, such as mulls, nun's-vailings, etc., are used in the construction. The over-dress may contrast with the skirt in color, fabric or pattern, as desired; figured goods being often combined with plain material in such costumes. The pattern for this costume is for misses from eight to fifteen years of age.

The *mousquetaire* hat is simply trimmed with a narrow band of velvet ribbon and two cockatoos artistically perched at the right side.

1883
Misses' Costume

This costume consists of Misses' basque No. 8668, over-skirt No. 8667, and skirt No. 8082 represented — The charm of this costume is the simplicity of its fashioning and decoration. The material is plaid zephyr gingham. The skirt is of the four-gored style, and is decorated at the foot with two deep flounces of embroidery. The mode is adapted to dress goods of all varieties, whether cotton, silk or woolen.

The over-skirt is especially adapted to washable goods, its shaping and draping are so simple and pretty. It comprises three gores and a full breadth, and is handsomely draped at each side-back seam by three deep plaits turning upward. These plaits cross-wrinkle the front gracefully and make the back stylishly *bouffant*, and may be easily let down when laundering becomes necessary. Lawns, percales, nainsooks, pongees, foulards, checked silks, etc., will be made up in this shape; and lace, embroidery, flat bands, braids or under-facings may complete its edges.

MISSES' COSTUME.

The basque flares in deep V-fashion below its closing of buttons and buttonholes, and is superbly fitted by single bust and under-arm darts, low side-back gores and a well curved center seam. It arches slightly high at the sides, and its back describes a pretty oval outline. Lace turns upward from the wrists of the coat sleeves, and a military collar encircles the high neck. It is a jaunty mode for white, colored and figured wash goods, and also for Summer silks and woolens of all pretty varieties. Lace or embroidery may turn upward from its edges; or a pretty application of braid may be employed as ornamentation when the finish illustrated is considered too simple for the fabric.

All three patterns were designed for misses from eight to fifteen years of age.

1883 Misses'
Work Apron

No. 8680. — This apron is not only as practical in purpose as its title suggests, but is also very ornamental in effect, and the union of these two attributes renders the pattern a most desirable one. Gingham, showing a commingling of dark and light blue, old-gold, white and cardinal, is the material selected for the construction in the present instance and the finish is appropriately very plain. The front of the apron is cut on a lengthwise fold of the goods and the waist and lower portion is in one piece for some distance back of the center at each side. The division between the upper and lower portion is made by a crosswise slash cut at the waistline and extending quite a distance in front of the underarm seams, all the additional width requisite for the front skirt portion of the garment being allowed back of the slash at each side. The back of the body portion is finished with hems at the closing edges and is closed with buttonholes and celluloid buttons. The seams upon the shoulders and under the arms give the requisite adjustment, and to the lower edge of the back at each side is subsequently sewed the corresponding half of the back skirt, which consists of a straight breadth that is seamed to the adjoining edge of the front. The top of this breadth and the edge of

8680
Front View.

8680
Back View.

the front below the slash are reduced to the proper size by gathers, which are regulated so that the back edges do not quite meet at the center. The top of the gathered portion is sewed to a narrow facing, which is felled at its upper edge to the body of the garment. This facing is continued to the closing, upon the under side is applied a similar facing. A deep hem lends an appropriate completion to the lower edge of the skirt. Narrow bindings finish the arms-eyes, no sleeves being added. About the neck is a pretty collar, the effect of which proves that becomingness in ordinary attire is not

difficult to achieve. It is formed of a straight strip of the material shirred twice about an inch from the top, the edge above the shirring forming a pretty ruffled finish. The collar is sewed to the neck of the garment through the shirrings and its ornamental effect is well worth the slight labor required in its arrangement.

Such aprons are almost indispensable to the protection of the toilette for a miss who paints, models or takes practical lessons in the no less fashionable art of housekeeping.

Pattern No. 8680 is suitable for misses from eight to fifteen years of age.

1883 Girls' Costume

No. 8674. — Sheer, fine lawn is the fabric of which this charming little toilette is made. The skirt is in box-plaited style and is sewed to a waist that is closed in front with buttons and buttonholes and nicely shaped by center, side and shoulder seams. The lower part of each box-plait is overlaid with a frill of fine open-work embroidery headed by a row of similar insertion: the result produced being quaint yet very pretty. The over-dress has three box-plaits stitched in its front, which is attached to a yoke that closes with button-holes and buttons. A slash is made under the left side of the center box-plait nearly to the waistline, and a button-stand is sewed to the left side, the closing being made with button-holes and buttons in a continuation of the yoke closing. At the waistline short slashes are made under the box-plaits; through these slashes is run a ribbon which has its ends tacked to the side seams under prettily made bows. These seams, a center seam and long underarm darts conform the over-dress gracefully to the figure, the side seams being left open a short distance at the bottom. The back-shapes two pretty points at the lower edge and is deepened and made quite orna-mental by similarly pointed tabs sewed flatly to its points underneath. The points and tabs are trimmed with lace headed by a row of insertion; a similar garniture is applied to the lower edge of the front. A row of insertion overlies the seam joining the yoke to the front and a ruche of lace affords a dainty finish for the neck. The coat sleeves are decorated to correspond with the remainder of the over-dress.

For combinations of silk and nun's-vailing or cashmere, two kinds of silk or two kinds of wool goods, the mode is as beautiful and stylish as it is for all sorts of white, colored and printed cottons. Lace or embroi-dery, ribbon, little ruffles, flat bands, braids, etc., are pretty and suitable decorations and may be disposed in any way pleasing to the taste.

Young girls from three to nine years of age will be attractively costumed in this outfit.

The coquettish hat has a full facing of silk nearly covering its much-rolled brim, and a wreath of wild roses about its crown.

Figure No. 7. — GIRLS' COSTUME.

8674
Front View.

8674
Back View.

1883
Girls' Costume

No. 8664. — A back view of this dainty little costume is given at Girls' Figure No. 8, the material and trimming both different from those here illustrated.

The fashion is especially commendable for wash goods, and the material represented in the present instance belongs to this class, the trimming being colored embroidery of a corresponding shade. The front of the dress is in Princess shape, with a bust dart and an underarm dart in each side; the back is also cut on a fold of the goods at its lower part and has a curved opening through the center of the body portion, which is under-faced with the material and provided with button-holes and buttons for the closing. Extra width is allowed below the closing and also at the same point upon the front edges of the back, and is folded underneath to give the effect of two broad box-plaits on the outside and contribute the necessary fullness to the skirt portion of the dress. The sleeves are in coat style and are prettily shaped to the arms. There is a standing band or choker collar about the neck, and outside of this is worn a deep, round collar which is narrowly under-faced at the neck edge and is remov-able. The removable collar and the wrists of the sleeves are each trimmed with a single row of embroidery and the bottom of the dress is ornamented with two rows as far as the plaits in the back, the upper one on the skirt portion and the frills on the sleeves being set on under tiny bands of the material.

Very often the deep collar will be entirely of embroidery and the sleeves will be cut from web embroidery or formed of strips of insertion joined together. This will, of course, be done only when the costume is made of fine goods and intended for best wear. A pretty dress is of plaid gingham; its trimming is rick-rack edging. Another is of bunting, the deep collar is of lace, the sleeves are completed with turn-back cuffs of lace and a row of lace is sewed flatly beneath the bottom of the skirt and turned upward upon the outside. The pattern will attain its greatest popularity during the coming season for gingham and other washable goods, the ease with which it may be laundered making it especially desirable for this class of fabrics.

Pattern No. 8664 is suitable for girls from three to nine years of age.

Figure No. 8. — GIRLS' OUTDOOR COSTUME.

8664
Front View.

8664
Back View.

1883
Child's Costume

No. 8660. — Although called a costume, the garment will be as often, perhaps even more frequently, worn as a cloak. It is, however, in every way adapted to the purposes of a costume and will usually be made of costume fabrics. Piqué is the material represented in this instance and embroidery in two widths, with insertion to match, constitutes the trimming. The body of the garment is not quite close-fitting and is very prettily proportioned by side-back seams and a center seam, all three of which terminate a little below the waistline. Extra width is allowed at the extremity of each of these seams and folded underneath to form a narrow box-plait between two wider box-plaits, the effect on the outside being that of two box-plaits between two backward-turning side-plaits. The folds of the side-plaits are slip-stitched to those of the box-plaits for a little below the ends of the actual side-back seams. This portion of the costume is deepest at the back, where it describes a decided point and then curves upward over the hips. In front of the underarm seams it maintains a uniform outline and the front is closed with buttonholes and buttons, the right side being hemmed and the left under-faced. A flounce, graduated in depth in proportion to the outline of the body portion, is cut from deep embroidery and narrowly hemmed at its front ends, while its top is scantily gathered from the front edges as far as the fold of the first plait in each side of the back. Back of this the folds of the plaits make sufficient fullness; and, as the flounce, after being sewed to the body portion, is headed by a row of insertion, the characteristic outlines of the mode are very prettily emphasized. The insertion, instead of being extended entirely across the front, is turned and carried up each side of the closing with pretty effect. The sleeves are in coat shape and are completed with full frills of embroidery set on under tiny bands. A narrow under-facing finishes the neck.

The removable cape mentioned in the title is cut from the wide embroidery and is shirred several times at its upper edge to adapt it to the size of the costume about the neck, the shirrings being sewed through to a fitted stay. A straight band of the material or a standing frill of narrow embroidery may finish the neck, the band being usually omitted when the frill is added.

When wide embroidery is employed, the dress material will not be used at all for the skirt portion. The cape may also be cut from the material, but is much more effective when made of the embroidery. Surah, silk, cashmere and similar textures will often be selected for such garments, and their trimmings will be laces and embroideries. The flounce may be cut with the front end on a fold when it is desired to close the front for its entire length.

This child's costume is appropriate for children two to six years old.

CHILD'S STREET COSTUME.

8660
Front View.

8660
Back View.

Figure No. 2. — CHILD'S DRESS.

8648
Front View.

8648
Back View.

1883
Child's Dress

No. 8648. — At Child's Figure No. 2, this dress is represented in plain suit goods, with checked velvet for the belt straps and cuff-facings.

The style of the dress is charming and is easily developed in any material adapted to girls' wear. Checked gingham is represented in the present instance and white embroidery forms the trimming. The front is cut on a fold of the goods at the center and is laid in five narrow box-plaits with about half an inch of space between each two plaits. These plaits are stitched in their folds from their top to some distance below the waistline, and below this they are allowed to fall out free. The upper portion of the back is in yoke shape and is laid in box-plaits matching those of the front in size and number. The plait at the center is made in the right half and the buttonholes for the closing are made through it, while the opposite side is turned

under for a hem and has the buttons sewed upon it. The yoke is nearly straight across its lower edge and to each half is sewed the corresponding half of the back proper. The closing of the latter is made with buttonholes and buttons, the right side being hemmed and the left under-faced. In each side, just back of the closing and turning toward it, are five tucks which are stitched to position to about the same depth as the plaits in the front, the fullness falling out gracefully below. The seams upon the shoulders and under the arms, aided by the tucks and plaits, give a stylish and easy adjustment to the dress; belt straps of the material, cut bias and bordered with narrow embroidery, are sewed upon the front at the waistline beneath the folds of the outermost plaits and fastened at the back with three buttons and buttonholes. A row of wider embroidery trims the bottom of the dress and the wrists of the coat-shaped sleeves. At the neck is a standing frill of embroidery, and upon the lower edge of the yoke embroidery is applied to form a pretty finish.

A dress of this style made of white lawn has very fine *torchon* lace for trimming. Another of pink nun's-vailing has ties of pink ribbon instead of the belt sections, its garnitures are Moresque lace and a knot of pink ribbon, the latter being fastened upon the left shoulder. The pattern will be as popular for lawns, mulls, nainsooks and other fine textures as it is for the coarser fabrics in vogue for play dresses; the garnitures will be varied to suit the material made up, and the uses of the garment. There is probably no material that wears out more gracefully than Scotch gingham and, as it can be purchased in all colors and in plain and figured variety, it is especially commendable for children's wear. It is trimmed with white and colored embroidery and with any other garniture that can be neatly applied to white fabrics.

The dress made from Pattern No. 8648 can be worn by children from one to six years of age.

1883 Child's Slip (Dress)

No. 8665. — By referring to Child's Figure No. 1, the effect of this slip, developed in plain blue chambrey, with embroidered muslin for the yoke portions, may be observed.

Nainsook is the material pictured in the present instance; embroidered edging and insertion form the trimming. The body of the slip is loose in its adjustment and has seams under the arms and very short seams upon the shoulders, being cut out in Pompadour fashion at both the front and back, where the openings are filled in with correspondingly shaped yoke-sections. The closing edges of the back yoke-sections are turned under in hems of equal width and united with buttonholes and tiny lace buttons; below these a lengthwise slash is made in the center of the back proper to lengthen the opening sufficiently, its edges being narrowly hemmed. The upper edges of the front and back are gathered to reduce them to the proper dimensions before being sewed to the yoke portions, and the fullness thus produced falls loosely in Greenaway fashion. Upon the bottom of the slip is a row of wide edging and a little above this is a row of insertion. The sleeves are in coat shape and are trimmed in exact harmony with the skirt, the edging being set on under a tiny band of the material in each instance. The yoke portions are composed entirely of strips of insertion joined together, and all their edges, the neck included and the closing excepted, are bordered with edging narrower than that on other portions of the garment, but set on in the same way under a very narrow strip of the material.

Slips of this style are among the most comfortable and becoming modes for little people and will be made of all kinds of seasonable fabrics worn by children. Ginghams in plain colors, checks, small plaids, etc., and prints and percales in pinhead dots and tiny floriated designs are liked for every-day wear; but white goods are preferred for more select occasions. Colored embroidery may be obtained to match all the fashionable tints, and white embroidery is procurable in all grades and widths. Cashmeres and nun's-vailings in dainty tints will be made up in this fashion, with lace or embroidered insertion for the yoke, and corresponding garnitures for the sleeves and lower edge.

Children from one to six years of age are appropriately dressed in Pattern No. 8665.

Figure No. 1. — CHILD'S SLIP.

8665
Front View.

8665
Back View.

1883 Child's Apron

No. 8675. — This apron, made of cross-barred muslin, with ruffles of embroidery and bands of insertion for trimming, is illustrated at Child's Figure No. 5.

Cambric is the material represented in the present instance, and the construction of the garment is so ornamental in itself that the small amount of trimming added sets it off to very good advantage. The front is cut on a fold of the goods at the center, and the back is folded underneath in hems at the closing edges. Both back and front are extended in narrow *bretelle* fashion over the shoulders, where they are united in short seams. Between the *bretelle* portions the apron is cut out in Pompadour shape, exposing the dress about the neck in a very pretty and graceful fashion. The seams under the arms are sprung out toward the lower edge so as to amplify the width symmetrically; upon the bottom of the garment is a wide gathered ruffle of the material edged with embroidery. Buttons and buttonholes close the back, and into the underarm seams a little below the waistline are sewed hemmed ties of the material. The inserted ends of these ties are each slightly narrowed by a shallow plait, while their free ends are trimmed with a narrow frill of the material edged with embroidery, and tied in sash style across the back. Overlying each *bretelle* portion is a band of insertion, which is carried in a point down the back and front to a little below the arms'-eyes. Narrow edging borders the insertion on both sides, that on the outer edge forming the finish for the upper portion of the arm's-eye. The tops of the front and back are similarly finished; upon the center of the front and the overlapping sides of the closing are arranged pointed strips of insertion matching those upon the *bretelles*, being like them pointed at their lower extremities and bordered with edging. The arms'-eyes are completed without sleeves, their lower parts being bordered with embroidery which meets that on the outer edge of the *bretelle* at each side.

Such aprons will be made of nainsook, lawn, print, linen and all kinds of washable goods and bordered with *torchon* lace, rick-rack, star braid, narrow ruffling or any other admired garniture. White aprons are considered most desirable by many ladies, as they cannot fade but there are many pretty prints and ginghams, that with proper care, may be frequently laundered without injury.

This costume is suitable for children from one to six years of age.

Figure No. 5. —
CHILD'S HOME COSTUME.

8675
Front View.

8675
Back View.

1883
Child's Dress

No. 8663. — The material used for this little costume is plain zephyr gingham, and the decoration consists of white cotton braid arranged in uniform rows. The garment has gores to the shoulders at the front and back, and between the side-front seams the front presents a narrow *plastron* effect. The gores at the back and also the center-backs extend only enough below the waistline to produce a graceful, long-waisted appearance. To the bottom of the short portion is attached a full skirt that is shirred several times near the top to form an ornamental and ruffled heading. The shirrings are stayed to the bottom of the body; the sides of the skirt are joined to the corresponding edges of the side-front gores. Three rows of braid surround the bottom of the dress and three similar rows trim the wrist of the sleeve. The neck is decorated with a deep collar in two parts, its ends flaring at the back and front and its edges being prettily trimmed with two rows of braid. Little ruffles of fine nainsook are

worn at the neck and wrists, and buttonholes and buttons close the garment at the back.

When white goods — which are especially charming for such dresses — are used, rows of insertion may cover the side-front and side-back seams, or the center-front may be of embroidered muslin to heighten its *plastron*-like appearance. Frills of lace may elaborate the skirt and sleeves, and the collar may be formed of insertion or embroidered muslin to correspond with the insertion near the seams or the fabric of the center-front. Colored goods, whether plain or figured, or of cotton, silk or woolen texture, are equally adapted to the mode; the trimming may be whatever the taste of the maker deems suitable for the fabric selected. Ribbons may be knotted across the front from the side-front seams with decidedly pretty effect, or they may be added in any manner considered becoming to the wearer.

The little cap (No. 7189) is of cloth, and is a fashion much admired for children of both sexes.

This garment can be appropriately worn by children from two to eight years old.

8663
Front View.

CHILD'S DRESS.

8663
Back View.

1883
Girls' Costume

No. 8769. — Cashmere is the fabric illustrated in the construction in the present instance; silk bands and a ribbon bow form the trimming. The skirt is in the much admired kilt style and has a plain yoke top, which is fitted smoothly about the hips and sewed to the belt, one end being turned under in a wide hem and lapped broadly upon the other at the back. To the lower edge of the yoke is joined the kilt composed of straight breadths joined together, turned under in a deep hem at the lower edge and laid in side-plaits all turning one way at the top, a slash being made beneath the plait at the center of the back to increase the length of the placket opening. A single tape, tacked to the under side of the plaits about one-third of the distance from the top, is the only means necessary, in addition to a good pressing, to hold them in position.

The body of the costume is like a loose-fitting jacket, with added vest-fronts. The latter are closed their depth with buttonholes and buttons — the right side being hemmed and the left under-faced — and are slightly pointed at the end of the closing. The fronts proper are considerably deeper than the vest, and, instead of meeting in the usual manner, extend no nearer the closing than the top of the shoulder seams, the space between the corresponding edges revealing the vest in a very attractive manner. Each side forms a decided point at its front edge below the vest, and then curves high over the hip and deepens again toward the underarm seam. There is an underarm dart in each side of the jacket front, and at the back are side-back seams and a center seam. Each side-back and its adjoining center-back form a deep and decided point below the waistline; this variation in the outline of the garment is especially attractive. The vest fronts are sewed with the jacket portions at their shoulder edges to the back, and their underarm edges are included in the underarm darts. A band of silk passes down each jacket front just back of its front edge and continues entirely about the lower edge, emphasizing the beauty of the lower outline in the most attractive manner. Beneath the double points at the back is fastened a large sash-bow of ribbon, which falls with the utmost grace. There is a straight band of choker collar about the neck, and in the same seam is sewed a deep sailor-collar with curved ends which is trimmed with a band of silk of the same width as those on the jacket. The sleeves are in coat shape and are handsomely completed with cuff facings of silk, the ends of which are slanted off at their upper edges and lapped upon the upper side under buttons.

8769
Front View.

8769
Back View.

Costumes of this style will often be made of two materials, one variety being used for the vest, the sailor collar and sometimes for the kilt, while the other will form the jacket portion. A pretty costume is made of plaid suiting and plain serge of the same tint as the ground shade in the plaid. The plaid is used for the vest, the collar, and cuff-facings and is applied in a broad bias band upon the kilt before the plaits are laid. Another costume is of dark blue flannel and the kilt is trimmed with three rows of narrow mohair braid, the same number being added upon all the jacket edges, including the sailor collar and the wrists of the sleeves.

This attractive costume may be worn by girls from three to twelve years of age.

8778
Front View.

8778
Back View.

1883
Girls' Costume

No. 8778. — This costume is as practical as it is pretty. Its adaptability to all varieties of dress goods worn by girls will at once establish its popularity. Plaid suit goods are illustrated in the present instance; a plaiting of the same with silk facings and pipings constitutes the trimming. The body of the costume is fitted by seams upon the shoulders and under the arms and a curving seam at the center of the back, and is fashionably long-waisted, extending some distance below the waistline. Buttons and buttonholes are used in closing it, the right side being hemmed and the left under-faced. There are three gores and a back breadth united in the skirt, which is short in proportion as the body portion is long; the gores are joined without any fullness while the back breadth is gathered. After the skirt and body have been joined together, the pretty drapery characterizing the mode is added. It consists of two sections, each of which is shaped to form the vest-like appliance upon one side of

the front and the panier portion below the hip. The top of the vest portion is shirred three times at its shoulder edge and is sewed in with the shoulder seam of the garment, its front edge extending nearly to the closing and being slip-stitched to position, while its back edge is piped with silk and invisibly sewed through this piping. At the extremity of the lengthwise or vest portion is made another cluster of three crosswise shirrings; back of these the upper edge of the panier portion is sewed to the body of the costume with a slightly descending inclination toward the center seam of the back, where the end of each panier is laid in a cluster of three upturning plaits. The lower edges of the paniers are piped with silk; a bow of ribbon is fastened over their plaited ends at the back. Upon the bottom of the skirt is a double box-plaiting of the material, under-faced with silk for about two inches at the top. This plaiting is set on to form its own heading and each plait is caught down from the top in shell shape to display the lining. A bias band of plaid, piped at both edges with silk, trims the coat-shaped sleeve; a choker

collar, also piped with silk, adds a tasteful finish to the neck. The remaining item in the decorations consists of a bow of ribbon which conceals the lower shirrings in the vest portions.

Two materials will often be united in a costume of this style — one being used for the draperies and skirt and sleeve garnitures and the other for the remainder of the costume. A pretty costume is made of blue and white Oxford check with plain blue for the drapery and trimmings. Another is of dark brown flannel with pipings, ribbon and buttons of red. Any diaphanous material may be made to present a variety of effects by having slips of different color to wear beneath and ribbons to match each set. The expense of such slips need be but trifling as they may be made of silk-finished Silesia.

This pattern is designed to be worn by girls from three to nine years of age.

1883
Childs' Costume

No. 8770. — Novel and dainty in effect, yet very simple in construction, this little costume is especially charming for afternoon or party wear. The material is foulard silk of a pretty flowered pattern and shell pink hue. The costume is composed of a body and skirt; over the skirt is arranged a flounce of deep Valenciennes lace which is headed by a cascade of similar lace in a much narrower width. The narrower lace also turns upward from the wrist of the coat sleeve and falls in a full frill about the neck. Wide ribbons, disposed in butterly bows upon the shoulders, pass down the sides of the front and back, their lower ends being fastened in single loops and prettily notched ends at the joining of the lace flounce. The disposal of the ribbons is novel and dressy. Side and shoulder seams give the body of the costume a graceful, clinging appearance; buttons and buttonholes close the back.

This pattern can be adapted to dress goods of all kinds including velvets, silks, Surahs, cashmeres, etc. On costumes of these fabrics lace or embroidery may be lavished with elaborate results or simple garnitures of the costume material or of contrasting goods may be used with very pretty effect. Handsome dresses of this style are made of embroidered muslin or lace net, worn over slips of silk finished Silesia or of silk, Surah, satin, etc.

Children from ages two to six will look attractive in this costume.

8770
Front View.

8770
Back View.

1884
Ladies' Costume

No. 9503. — The fabrics employed in its development are Kursheedt's Standard all-over embroidered Cheviot in Gordon blue, with the embroidery of a deep wine color, and plain velvet of the same deep wine tone. About the front of the round walking-skirt is a narrow side-plaiting sewed on to form a self-heading; this is the only garniture added to the skirt. Upon the gores are arranged two deep draperies which are plaited up closely at their front edges near the top — where they are seamed — and then flare widely from the center of the front to fall in deep points nearly to the foot of the skirt, plaits clustered high up in the back edges completing the draping in a stylish manner.

The fitting of the over-dress is close and handsome, and is made by center and side-back seams and underarm and bust darts. The fronts of the over-dress fall in short, round *paniers* over the front-draperies, the *paniers* being plaited up at their front and back edges. The back-drapery falls deep and square almost to the edge of the skirt; its width is very much increased by extra fullness left at the lower end of the center seam and at the front edges. Its center is looped up to the center seam, and its front edges are plaited near the top into the side-back seams below the waistline, deep, downward-turning plaits in the lower front edges and tackings to the skirt completing the full draping. An officer's collar of the plain material encircles the neck, and deep, round cuffs are simulated with the plain material on the coat sleeves, which are gathered at the top to stand becomingly high at the shoulders.

Embroidery in tints contrasting with the ground shade is conspicuous on many of the novelty textures of the season, and the designs are neat and frequently very pretty; these embroidered fabrics are combined with silk, Surah, velvet, velveteen, plush, etc., or with the same texture showing a plain finish. The mode illustrated is particularly effective for such combinations, and the skirt may be garnitured to please the fancy, narrow and elaborate decorations being both suitable. A simple finish is much preferred for these fabrics, but for silks and other dress goods to which the mode is also well adapted, laces, *passementeries*, braids, *appliqué* embroideries, etc., may be selected, with rich effect. Velvet is fashionable in combination with all textures and may be used in large or small quantities and in any way preferred. Fur may be selected to garniture costumes of this style, with rich effect, being disposed to please the taste.

The hat is of fine felt, handsomely trimmed with velvet and a large bird that is placed directly in front.

LADIES' COSTUME.

9503
Front View.

9503
Side-Back View.

1884 Ladies' Trained Costume

No. 9482. — This costume is developed in a combination of plain and brocaded dress goods; the contrast is effectively brought out by the method of construction. The petticoat, as it is customary to call the short skirt of a trained toilette, is composed of three gores and a full back-breadth, the gores being fitted smoothly about the hips by darts and the breadth gathered to the proper size. Upon the upper portion of the gores are arranged hip-draperies, which are of uneven dimensions and especially attractive in their arrangement. The wider one is draped by five upturning plaits in its back edge, and is drawn up still higher at its front edge by a row of shirring that extends from the lower edge nearly to the top. It is applied upon the skirt with its back edge even with the right side-back seam — into which it is sewed — and its front edge at the left side-front seam, into which this edge is also sewed. The narrower drapery is lifted at its back edge by three overlapping, upward-turning plaits just below the hip, and its front edge is entirely undraped and overlaps the shirred end of the opposite drapery. Both draperies are conformed to the gores by darts, and the front end of the narrower one is sewed into the seam of the dart nearest the shirred end of the wider one. Both draperies are rounded gracefully at their lower edges, and the inequality of their dimensions adds a novel feature to their *panier* effect. Extending from beneath them are two fan-plaited ornaments which are sewed at their front edges into the side-front seams and slip-stitched invisibly at their back edges upon the side-gores. Each of these ornaments consists of an oblong section which is turned under for a hem at the bottom and laid in three backward-turning plaits that overlap each other at the top and flare toward the lower edge. A tape, tacked to the plaits underneath about a third of their distance from the bottom, holds them securely in their folds. These fans fall even with the bottom of the skirt, and between them and back of them the depth is slightly decreased by turning under the lower edge in a hem about two inches wide, a very tasteful finish being imparted by adding a foot-plaiting of corresponding depth. The foot-plaiting, the fan-ornaments and the hip-draperies are of plain goods.

The train is of ample width and superb length, with a graceful oval outline that is especially becoming. The requisite dimensions for it are obtained by joining together breadths of the goods, and the fullness of the top is gathered into the proper size, and both train and hip-draperies are sewed with the

9482

Right Side-Front View, showing the Costume with Fancy Sleeves of Demi-Length and the Neck cut out in Pompadour Style.

9482

Left Side-Back View, showing the Costume with Full-Length Sleeves and a High Neck.

skirt to the belt, the placket opening being finished at the left side. The side edges of the train are included in the side-back skirt seams to within a short distance of the bottom, and a lining of plain goods is added to the lower portion, while the edge is underlaid with a *balayeuse* of Swiss. Tackings are made through the train to the skirt a little below the belt to prevent its fullness from spreading beyond a fashionably narrow limit; tapes or elastics are sewed beneath the side-back seams and adjusted as closely to the figure as may be becoming. Lace borders the hip-draperies.

The body of the costume is in basque style and is deeply and fashionably pointed at the center of the front and back. It closes in front with buttonholes and buttons, the right side being hemmed and the left underfaced. In each side two bust darts are taken; the remainder of the adjustment is perfected by means of underarm gores, side-back seams and a center seam, the three back seams being sprung out so as to give as much spring below the waistline as is required by the train. One view of the costume shows the sleeve finished with a frill of lace, the material being cut away from under the lace; the other displays it cut off to elbow length, slashed twice across the top, and shirred through the center, between, above and below the slashes to form two diamond-shaped openings, which reveal the arm in a dressy manner. These openings are bordered

with narrow lace, and the lower edge of the sleeve is finished with a frill of the wider variety. This view showing the fancy sleeve also represents the neck cut out square in front and trimmed with a frill of narrow lace turning inward and upward and a frill of the wider variety having the opposite effect. In this view the materials are represented in light colors. Another view shows the neck completed with a ruche of deep lace outside a high standing collar, and the fabrics are represented in dark colors.

Of course, the selection and arrangement of contrasting fabrics in a costume of this style are regulated entirely by personal taste, the train and basque being of plain goods and the remainder of brocade. Sometimes the hip-draperies will be made of lace or embroidered Brussels net, and the sleeves will be of the same or perhaps will be omitted altogether. A beaded, embroidered or hand-painted front-gore may be applied, with elegant results; or the side-gores may be beaded, embroidered or painted to suggest panels, and lace, beaded or not, in any preferred variety may be selected. A superb costume for a bride is made of cream-white satin and embroidered *crêpe de Chine*, the latter material forming the gores and hip-draperies. Plain demi-length sleeves are chosen, and their wrists and the open neck are trimmed with *duchesse* lace. Matrons will admire the mode for black and colored fabrics.

1884
Misses' Costume

No. 9467. — In the present instance the costume is made of Middlesex flannel. The skirt is of the fashionable four-gored style; upon the gores is a straight drapery that is laid in five broad, triple box-plaits and extends from a little below the belt evenly with the bottom of the gores. Three rows of velvet ribbon of the same number of different widths trim the lower part of this drapery, arranged so that the widest row is at the bottom and the narrowest at the top. A narrow double box-plaiting trims the bottom of the back-breadth.

The over-dress is very handsomely fashioned. Its fronts open from the shoulders upon a short, pointed vest, which extends all the way under them and is buttoned from the throat to the lower edge. Two forward-turning plaits are folded in each front from the shoulder to the waistline, and are sewed along their under-folds to the vest. Below the vest the fronts are prolonged to form deep, pointed *paniers*, which are plaited up stylishly at their back edges. The vest is faced as far back as necessitated by the fronts with velvet, and is fitted by single bust and underarm darts, the underarm darts being taken up with corresponding darts in the fronts. Side-back seams and a center seam complete the adjustment and terminate in extra widths that amplify the drapery suitably. The side-back extra widths are underfolded in a forward-turning plait at each side, while the center extra width is caught up in three plaits on the center seam to produce the full bow-drapery so fashionable. Loopings to under-tapes below the side-back seams and deep downward-turning plaits in the front edges complete the high, *bouffant* draping of the back, which falls deep and square upon the skirt. An officer's collar is at the neck, and bows of many loops of satin ribbon are fastened at the throat and waistline over the closing of the vest. Three rows of narrow velvet ribbon encircle the wrists of the sleeves, and a button is placed on each row at the back of the wrist. A linen choker-collar is worn about the neck with neat effect.

This is a most dressy mode for evening and party wear when developed in suitable fabrics. All varieties of goods are adapted to it and combinations of two or more textures are very effective. Lace, embroidery, braid, *passementerie*, flat bands, etc., are suitable garnitures and may be applied to please the fancy, simple disposals being, however, most effective on costumes of this style. White silks or woolens with dark or bright-hued velvets are fashionable; and the unfriendliness of white to some complexions is easily overcome by the thicker fabric.

MISSES' COSTUME.

Pattern No. 9467 is suitable for misses from eight to fifteen years of age.

The coquettish hat is of fine felt with a puffed brim-facing of silk. It is trimmed with plumage and a rosette-bow of ribbon loops.

No. 9465. — Velvet is associated as a decorative accessory with plain dress goods in the construction of the costume in this instance, and the effect is especially attractive. The skirt comprises the usual gores and back-breadth in its construction, and the gores are fitted by darts, while the breadth is gathered in the usual manner. Upon the gores is adjusted a deep, oval *tablier*-drapery, which is also fitted by darts at its top and is lifted high at each side by a cluster of four upturning plaits. The back-drapery is a full breadth, which is gathered across the top and has three downward-turning plaits in each side. It is sewed in with the side-back seams for about two-thirds of its depth from the top, the side edges of the *tablier* being included in the same seams. The back-drapery has a single loose loop tacked in its center to complete the process of draping; its

9467
Side-Back View.

9467
Front View.

edges are plainly finished. A broad band of velvet borders the bottom of the *tablier* and a slightly broader band surmounts a tiny box-plaiting upon the skirt. Tapes, fastened beneath the side-back seams and tied together, regulate the closeness of the skirt to the figure; both skirt and drapery are sewed to the same belt, the placket opening being finished at the left side-back seam.

The body is in basque style and in the process of fitting single bust darts, underarm gores, side-back seams and a center seam are introduced. The lower edge curves upward over the hips and deepens in coat style at the back. The center seam is terminated a little below the waistline, the fullness at its extremity being underfolded in a double box-plait. The front is closed with button-holes and buttons, the right side being hemmed and the left underfaced; upon it is adjusted a removable Molière vest which is made of velvet and is turned in at the top and shirred across twice, a tiny bias underfacing serving as a stay. The side edges are turned under quite broadly, and the lower edge is gathered once and finished with a narrow binding. Three crosswise rows of shirring are made at the waistline and stayed by a narrow band that is sewed underneath. In adjusting the vest upon the basque, it is attached invisibly at the neck. The lower end is folded up underneath so as to conceal the binding and attached in the same way. A long, fancy clasp appears to hold the waist-line shirrings in position. A standing collar and deep, round cuff-facings of velvet complete the neck and sleeves.

As the vest is removable, it may be omitted in favor of any other style of ornament preferred. Such a vest is, however, almost universally becoming to misses, and will as a general rule be retained. Ribbons

9465
Front View.

9465
Side-Back View.

may be tied across its waistline and neck shirrings, and the dress goods may, if preferred, be used in its construction. Costumes of this style will be made up for dancing, church and school wear, their

purpose determining their materials and trimmings, though the most ceremonious occasion at which young people are likely to be present does not invite, nor even excuse, over-ornamentation.

1884
Girls' Dress

No. 9448. — This costume is represented in cashmere in Figure No. 9.

Gray cashmere is charmingly associated with ruby velvet in the present instance, the velvet being used for the yoke, which is of becoming depth and has seams upon its shoulders, its back edges being hemmed and closed with buttonholes and buttons. To the edges of the yoke is sewed the deeper portion of the garment, which is cut on a fold of the goods at the front and back and has shapely seams at the sides. A slash, extending some distance from the top, is made at the center of the back; the shape of the lower part of the arms'-eyes is cut from the sides above the tops of the seams. The upper edges are turned in for a finish and three rows of shirring are made in the front and in each side of the back. The shirrings are only about a quarter of an inch apart, and below the waistline five rows, extending entirely about the figure, but having most of their fullness concentrated at the front and back, are made at intervals of about half an inch. These shirrings are sewed through to a fitted stay, and the upper shirrings are stayed by being sewed upon the yoke. The lower shirrings adjust the dress prettily to the figure without rendering it close-fitting, and they are as well adapted to cotton as to

Figure No. 9. —
GIRLS' SHIRRED DRESS.

9448
Front View.

9448
Back View.

woolen goods. Enough extra length is allowed below them to form the skirt and permit of three inch-wide tucks above a hem of medium width. The tucks are stitched in their folds and the hem is also stitched, the effect being quite decorative. Each sleeve is composed of a single section that is sloped off toward the wrist, its lengthwise edges being joined by a seam at the inside of the arm. Its lower edge is also sloped off slightly toward the extremity of this seam, and is underfaced with the goods and drawn into a frill about the hand by two rows of shirring made about two inches from the margin.

The shirrings are tacked to a stay and the top of the sleeve is gathered slightly before being sewed into the arm's-eye, thus forming a pretty curve over the shoulder. A straight collar, inside which a frill of lace is basted, finishes the neck.

It will be readily understood how many very attractive contrasts and comminglings may be united in a dress of this shape. Any becoming color may be used for the yoke, and also for the sleeves, if desired. Lace or embroidery, or braid in parallel lines, may be arranged below the tucks; but a plain hem is just as suitable a finish. If the tucks be not

desired, the length necessary for them may be deducted in cutting out the dress. A pretty illustration of the mode is developed in white cashmere, with pale blue for the yoke, the latter portion being overlaid with Irish point embroidery. The tucks and hem are feather-stitched with pale blue floss, and upon one shoulder is a *caresse* — a bow composed of medium long loops and ends — of pale blue ribbon.

Pattern No. 9448 is for girls from three to nine years of age.

1884 Girls' Dress

The garment is particularly pretty and youthful in its style and will often be made up as a dancing-school toilette or for holiday wear. Plain dress goods are here united with Kursheedt's Standard lace tucking in its development and the effect is especially attractive. The *guimpe* is made of lace tucking and fitted by the seams upon the shoulders and at the sides. It is closed its depth at the back with concealed buttons and buttonholes, the right side being hemmed and the left underfaced. The neck is cut high and is finished with a narrow ruffle of lace. Full-length coat sleeves are sewed into the arms'-eyes, and their wrists are finished with ruffles of deeper lace. The waist is cut with bretelle-like extensions that reach over the shoulders, short seams joining the edges of the front and back; its front edges, instead of meeting, are separated by a broad space. Two straps of the material are

sewed to the left side and three to the right side. The edges are piped and the free ends are pointed and have buttonholes worked in them. Buttons are sewed upon the opposite sides of the waist and the buttonholes are slipped over them, the fronts being thus arranged in a very ornamental manner. The upper strap is some distance below the shoulder seams and the back is cut out in pompadour fashion to a corresponding depth. Side-back seams and a curving center seam give the most shapely and becoming proportions without rendering the adjustment too close. The arms'-eyes and neck edges, and also the edges to which the straps are sewed, are finished with piping. The skirt is formed of straight breadths joined together, turned under for a hem at the lower edge and laid in plaits turning from the center of the front. The top is sewed to the lower edge of the waist, and between the fronts it is sewed to belt sections that are sewed at their back ends to the waist, below

the lower straps. A placket opening is finished beneath the left side of the box-plait in the front, and all the plaits are pressed carefully to retain them in their folds. The joining of the skirt to the waist is concealed by a broad ribbon sash, which is passed about the figure and tied in a large bow at the back.

The effect of the costume when adjusted upon the figure is carefully shown in the engravng, and its appearance will suggest many dainty and becoming combinations that may be developed. The *guimpe* will often be of bright cashmere, Surah, velvet, etc., when the remainder is of pale or neutral-tinted goods. All kinds of open-worked goods are also in fashion for the *guimpe*. The sash may be of the dress goods, if the latter be of a soft texture, but Surah or ribbon is usually preferred for it.

Pattern No. 9472 is suitable for girls from three to nine years of age.

GIRLS' COSTUME.

9472
Front View.

9472
Back View.

1884
Misses' Costume

No. 9464. — Plain and brocaded silk are combined in the costume in the present instance and the result is exceedingly stylish. The four-gored skirt has a very broad double box-plaited panel of the brocade upon the center of the front, extending from the belt even with the lower edge. Back of the panel the gores are trimmed more than half-way to the belt with double box-plaitings of the plain silk alternating with ruffles of deep lace. At each side of the panel is arranged a deep, round drapery which is plaited up stylishly at its front and back edges. These draperies droop gracefully and are trimmed along the edges with frills of lace. Upon the back of the skirt is arranged a full drapery which is plaited to the belt and draped in two *bouffant* points by deep plaits in the front edges and loopings at the center. The lower three rows of trimming on the gores are continued across the back-breadth, and a ruffle of lace forms the edge garniture of the back-drapery.

Bust and underarm darts, side-form seams and a center seam perform the adjustment of the basque, the middle three seams of the back being left open for several inches at the bottom, allowing the center-backs to fall in two pretty tabs. The basque is deep and about uniform in outline all the way around. Buttons and buttonholes close it in front and a perfectly plain finish is observable at its edges. At the neck is an officer's collar which upholds a ruff of *lisse*. The coat sleeves are shortened slightly and are prettily completed by a full ruffle of lace at the edge and a full bow of ribbon fastened upon the upper side just over the lace.

The neck may be finished in any becoming manner, or lace may be applied in *jabots* or in flat rows upon the front with very pretty effect. Any combination of materials may be followed in costumes of this style, as the mode is well adapted to all seasonable fabrics. Velvet may be used in combination with any other material, whether silk or wool, plain or fancy. Any desired garniture may be added to the skirt, which may be simply or elaborately trimmed, as is most pleasing to the taste. Sometimes only a single row of trimming will be added to it, and this will be wide or narrow as preferred.

Pattern No. 9464 is for misses from eight to fifteen years of age.

MISSES' COSTUME.

9464
Front View.

9464
Side-Back View.

43

1884 Girls' Costume

No. 8840. — The construction of the costume quite closely simulates a polonaise and skirt, but requires less material in its development. Dress goods like a fine serge in texture are represented in the present engravings; ruffles of the same, soutache embroidery and ribbon bows constitute the garnitures. The foundation of the costume is in Princess style, the front being cut on a fold of the goods at the center and having side-front gores extending to the shoulders. In these gores are underarm darts; at the back are side-back gores curving into the arms'-eyes. The closing edges are slightly hollowed to assist in the adjustment and the closing is made with buttonholes and buttons from the neck to some distance below the waist-line; the overlapping side being under-faced, the underlapping side extended the width of a button-stand, and the edges below joined together in a seam. Upon each side of the front is arranged an ornamental portion, which sews into the shoulder seam and extends just far enough in front of the front-gore seam to conceal it. This section, previous to being draped, reaches nearly to the bottom of the skirt; the underarm dart is taken up through it to assist in conforming it to the garment. Its back edge is sewed in with the underarm seam to a little below the waistline. Then it is freed from the seam and the portions below are gradually narrowed into sash widths. A little back of the point where the drapery leaves the underarm seam, its upper edge is turned under for a finish and three upward-turning plaits are folded below, these plaits drawing the front edges backward and being firmly tacked over the side back seam. At the end of the closing the sash portions are shirred-up to a narrow width, crossed and sewed together through the shirrings, the free lengths being then tacked to form handsome loops and moderately long ends. A cross-piece with shirred ends is disposed over the crossing and tacked to the garment below its closing to give a neat effect. Three ruffles of the material, gathered and set on to form their own finish trim the skirt prettily; a tasteful design in soutache embroidery borders the front and the lower edge of each drapery portion. The sleeves are in coat shape and are trimmed at the wrists with soutache embroidery. About the neck is a close standing collar; beneath the front edges of the drapery portions at the shoulders and waistline are fastened ribbons, which are tied in pretty bows over the center-front.

8840
Front View.

8840
Back View.

All materials in vogue for girls' wear make up handsomely in this way, and the shape is so complete and pretty in itself that it will be a particular favorite. The over-lapping front edges may be under-faced with bright color, or cut in scallops and underlaid with lace, when a dressy effect is desired.

Quite an attractive effect it produced by facing the front proper between the over-lapping portions with contrasting material. The sash portions may also show a con-trasting lining.

Girls from three to nine years old may wear this costume.

1884
Girls' Costume

No. 9449. — This costume is represented in embroidered flannel, with silk for the drapery and lace about the wrists, at Girls' Figure No. 10.

Cashmere is the material here represented, and the pretty buttons which close the front and ornament the sleeves are the only garnitures added. The body is fashionably long-waisted and the fronts lap broadly. Their tops are extended to reach to the opposite shoulder seams and their closing edges are curved inward toward the waistline and outward below it. The right side overlaps the left and both edges are underfaced and the closing is continued along the shoulder edge of the overlapping side, while the underlapping extension is fastened to position at the shoulder by hooks and eyes. In each side is a shallow underarm dart, which gives a graceful adjustment without necessitating a close fit; at the back is a curving seam that produces a symmetrical effect. The skirt is short in proportion to the depth of the body portion and, while presenting the general effect of a kilt, is yet sufficiently different to be noticeable for its novelty. It is formed of straight breadths joined together, turned under for a hem at the lower edge and laid in clusters of overlapping plaits, there being three plaits in each cluster and quite a broad space allowed between every two. Over the seam joining the skirt to the body is sewed a sash-like drapery that is turned under for a hem at its upper edge and laid in three upturning plaits in each end. After being sewed to position, it is turned up over its own seam and its ends are sewed flatly upon the back just in front of the center seam. The sash effect is completed by means of a long, straight strip of the goods, hemmed broadly all around and shirred closely across its center. It is tacked upon the back of the costume so as to form a double-looped effect and two ends, and its disposal conceals the ends of the drapery portion previously described. A piece of the goods, cut bias and folded under for hems at its sides, is arranged in knot fashion over the shirring, its ends being tacked invisibly underneath. Four buttons trim the upper side of each of the coat sleeves and a high standing collar completes the neck.

Costumes of this shape are often made of two kinds of goods, one being used for the skirt and the other for the remainder. Velvets, velveteens, cloths and suitings of all kinds are adapted to the mode. Braid will often be applied as a garniture, but only flat decorations are in keeping with the style of the garment, and even they are not essential. The sash-drapery may be of contrasting goods when the remainder of the costume is of uniform texture. A pretty costume is made of gray cashmere, with deep cardinal Surah for the sash-drapery. The collar and wrists show pipings of the bright color.

Pattern No. 9449 has been designed for girls from three to nine years of age.

Figure No. 10. — GIRLS' COSTUME.

9449
Front View.

9449
Back View.

9479
Front View.

9479
Back View.

Figure No. 6. — GIRLS' COSTUME.

1884
Girls' Costume

No. 9479. — Girls' Figure No. 6 shows this costume made up in a combination of fancy wool goods and Surah, with facings of velvet and buttons or garnitures.

The mode is especially adapted to materials deemed appropriate for best wear, and is also suitable for those that are selected for general service. Dress goods were chosen for its construction in the present instance and facings of the same and velvet constitute the garnitures. The skirt is a kilt formed of straight breadths joined together, turned under for a wide hem at the lower edge and laid in box-plaits all around. It is sewed to a long-waisted body, which has seams upon the shoulders and an underarm gore between the front and back at each side, its closing edges being curved to assist in the adjustment, finished with under-facings and closed with buttonholes and buttons. Over the joining is arranged a sash of the goods, which is formed of a long, straight section that is tied in a bow at the back and held in position by being tacked through the knot and also through the center. A high standing collar of velvet finishes the neck of the waist, but no sleeves are added.

The jacket is especially jaunty and attractive in effect. Its fitting is accomplished by means of an underarm dart in each side of the front, a curving seam at the center of the back and the customary seams upon the shoulders and at the sides. Its front edges do not meet, but overlap ornamental sections of velvet which are sewed to position invisibly at their back edges and are joined as far as they extend at their shoulder edges with the fronts to the back. Extensions, allowed upon the upper parts of both the ornamental sections and jacket fronts, are turned back in lapels, below which the jacket edges are cut away with a slightly diagonal effect. The lapels of the ornamental portions are faced with velvet and those of the jacket fronts with the dress goods; a wide rolling collar of velvet meets the lapels in notches. The ornamental portions, instead of being closed, fall sufficiently apart to disclose the underwaist. The sleeves are in coat shape and are completed in harmony with the remainder of garment by having pointed cuff-facings of velvet applied to their wrists.

Soft Surah or wide ribbon may be chosen for the sash of such a costume but the material made up is just as suitable for the purpose. Plain and plaid or figured goods of any kind associate tastefully in a costume of this style. Sometimes the lapels, the collar and the wrists of the sleeves will be ornamented with crosswise or lengthwise lines of braid laid very close together.

This pattern is suitable for girls from five to twelve years of age.

9439
Front View.

9439
Back View.

GIRLS' COSTUME.

1884
Girls' Costume

No. 9439. — Velvet and watered silk were employed for the garment in this instance, satin and buttons being also introduced as decorative accessories. The fronts are cut the full depth of the garment, and from the top of the shoulder seams to the waistline are turned back in narrow, graduated lapels. Upon their back edges below the waistline are allowed extensions, the purpose of which will be explained later on. Beneath the fronts proper are adjusted under or vest fronts, which are sewed with the outer fronts to the back at the shoulder seams, and also at the underarm seams of the body portion as far down as the extra widths, below which they are joined flatly. Underarm gores, side-backs and a curving center seam divide the back, which extends but a little below the waistline, into the most shapely proportions; the depth is equalized

all around by the addition of a kilt-plaited skirt portion that is turned under for a hem at the lower edge and laid in plaits turning toward the center at the top. After this skirt portion is joined to the extensions allowed upon the back edges of the fronts, the first plait at each side is folded in the extension so as to conceal the joining. The fronts proper are turned under for hems at their lower edges, corresponding with those of the kilt; the vest sections, which are of watered silk, are closed their depth with buttonholes and crochet buttons. The outer fronts fall slightly apart below the ends of the lapels, buttons being sewed upon one side and buttonholes worked in the other, with very ornamental effect. Upon each front narrow bands of satin are arranged to simulate two perpendicular slashes with a narrow space between them; back of the slashes buttons are placed in line, while in front of them buttonholes are simulated with silk twist. Into the side seams at the waistline the plaited ends of wide ribbons are sewed and

their free ends are slanted off, carried to the back over the seam of the skirt and tied in a large sash-bow. The lapels are faced with satin and their tops underlap the ends of the satin-lined rolling collar in notches. The sleeves are in coat shape, and the upper side of each ornamented with two rows of buttons and simulated buttonholes.

While the combination of materials described in the present instance is very effective, it is not by any means essential to the perfect development of the costume. One material may be used throughout, or only two may be united, as preferred. The arrangement of the decoration shown in the present instance is particularly pretty and will very often be duplicated. The sash may be of the costume fabric or of whatever material is chosen for the facings, etc. Suitings, plushes, Surahs, etc., will be made up in this way.

Pattern No. 9439 is for girls from three to nine years of age.

1884
Child's Costume

No. 9426. — This costume is very attractively represented in a combination of cashmere and Surah in the same color, with lace for trimming, at Child's Figure No. 4.

Dress goods of a pretty but inexpensive quality are here used for the garment, and lace and a fancy pin constitute the garnitures, the sash being rendered all the more ornamental by being cut from ribbon. The body is fashionably long-waisted, and has seams upon the shoulders and at the sides. In the center of the front is folded and stitched a wide box-plait, and over the hem of the overlapping side of the back is a similar plait, the buttonholes and buttons performing the closing being thus concealed. To the lower edge is joined the skirt, which is formed of straight breadths joined together, turned under for a hem at the bottom and laid in groups of three narrow side-plaits alternating with single wide side-plaits. The plaits require only a careful pressing to hold them in their folds, and the variation from the usual style of kilt is very attractive and much admired for its novelty. Over the seam joining the skirt and body together is arranged the sash, its ends being brought to the back and tied in a large bow. A fancy pin is fastened through the center to hold it in position upon the costume. The sleeves are in coat shape and are completed with lace turned back in cuff fashion. A frill of lace is also sewed inside the little standing collar.

It is merely a matter of individual fancy whether the sash be made of ribbon or the dress goods, or of soft Surah or other appropriate contrasting material. It is equally a matter of taste whether the contrast be developed in the texture or color.

In the view of the costume given at Figure No. 4, the sash is shirred through the center and tacked to the dress through the shirring, and this arrangement will usually be followed when the sash is not made of ribbon. Two materials may be united in the construction with pleasing results, the kilt being of one kind and the remainder of another. A pretty costume has the body and sash of navy-blue cashmere and the skirt of dark cardinal.

This is an appropriate costume for children two to six years of age.

9426
Front View.

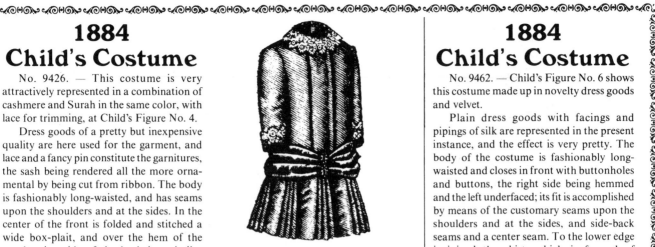

9426
Back View.

Figure No. 4. — CHILD'S COSTUME.

1884
Child's Costume

No. 9462. — Child's Figure No. 6 shows this costume made up in novelty dress goods and velvet.

Plain dress goods with facings and pipings of silk are represented in the present instance, and the effect is very pretty. The body of the costume is fashionably long-waisted and closes in front with buttonholes and buttons, the right side being hemmed and the left underfaced; its fit is accomplished by means of the customary seams upon the shoulders and at the sides, and side-back seams and a center seam. To the lower edge is joined the skirt, which is formed of straight breadths joined together and turned under for a wide hem at the lower edge. The top is laid in box-plaits and is sewed to the front and sides of the body a little above the lower edge of the latter. Between the side-back seams, however, the skirt is seamed flatly upon the body portion, with the tops of the two back plaits extending above the seam and forming a pretty heading that is rendered all the more attractive by a facing of silk. At each side, between the side-back seam and the closing, over the seam joining the skirt to the waist, is sewed an ornamental portion, which is cut in deep tabs and piped with silk. These ornaments fall over and conceal their own seams, and their addition imparts a sort of jacket effect that is very attractive and gives an air of completeness suggestive of street wear. A tape sewed to the under side of the skirt holds the plaits in their folds. The sleeves are in coat shape and are completed with pointed cuff-facings of silk. There is a high standing collar about the neck; in the same seam with it is sewed a round cape-collar which is cut in tabs smaller than but matching those of the ornamental portions on the skirt. The edges of the cape collar are piped with silk.

Costumes like this will be made of all materials worn by children. Fine flannels, soft cloths, plushes, velvets, cashmeres and white goods are all adapted to the mode. Sometimes the tabs will be bordered or underlaid with lace or embroidery, and sometimes they will be simply lined or bound with braid; the finish being regulated by the texture of the goods and the intended uses of the garment. A pretty costume of cream-white Cheviot has both collars and the skirt formed of velvet in a deep cardinal tone. The plaits at the back show a facing of the same color, and the sleeves have little found cuffs of the same. *Ecru* cloth or cashmere, with brown for its accessories, makes up stylishly.

Very appropriate for children from two to six years of age is Pattern No. 9462.

9462
Front View.

CHILD'S COSTUME.

9478
Front View.

9462
Back View.

9478
Back View.

Figure No. 6. — CHILD'S COSTUME.

1884
Child's Costume

No. 9478. — The material represented in the present instance is fancy Cheviot of a stylish blending of colors. The skirt comprises two gores and a gathered back-breadth and is joined to a long waist that is shaped by shoulder and underarm seams and is closed at the back. This waist is sleeveless and is usually of Silesia, muslin or some lining material, unless extra warmth is desired and then the dress fabric is used. A narrow box-plaiting of the material, finished to form a self-heading, trims the bottom of the skirt. The jacket has long underarm darts and three nicely curved seams to conform it gracefully to the figure, the center seam terminating at the top of an under-folded double box-plait, while at each side seam are underfolded two backward-turning plaits which give the back skirt the effect of two double box-plaits. The right front overlaps the left to the shoulder seam, from which it rounds away so that its lower corner comes below the right hip. The left front widens from the neck to a little below the waistline, to which point the garment is closed; below the closing it is cut away sharply, the result produced being very jaunty and stylish. Hooks and loops make the closing, and down the overlapping front edge is a wide band of plush, which is continued about the bottom of the front. The left front is trimmed at its lower edge with a similar band, which is continued up the front edge to the closing. A row of buttons is arranged along the closing just back of the band. Round cuffs are simulated on the coat sleeves with plush and a little standing band completes the neck.

Any simple *lingerie* may be worn with a costume of this style. All varieties of dress goods in vogue may be made up singly or in a combination of two or more materials. The skirt may be finished plainly, or it may be trimmed with lace, embroidery, ruffles, plaitings, etc., as most suited to its fabric. The jacket may be completed to correspond.

Pattern No. 9478 is for children from two to six years of age.

The hat has a velvet crown, and a brim of shirred satin ruffled at the edge. It is trimmed with ribbon.

1885 Ladies' Costume

No. 9667. — This exquisite costume is here made of golden-brown twilled cloth and seal-brown Jersey cloth, a side-plaiting of the former fabric and Kursheedt's Standard embroidered tinsel braid being effectively applied as garniture. The plaiting is about four inches deep and forms the foot decoration of the round walking-skirt, being set on to form a self-heading. Upon the left side of the gores is a broad panel that falls over the plaiting and is overlaid at equal intervals with cross-rows of the braid mentioned. The *tablier* is draped very high at the left side by wide plaits clustered in the left edge and deepens gradually, falling in a handsome point at the right side, where it is also draped high by plaits. The back-drapery falls in square outline almost to the foot of the skirt, and is very simply draped by a wide, downward-turning plait in each side edge and loopings at the center. Two rows of braid laid close together border the edges of the *tablier*, but the back-drapery is plainly finished.

The basque is very handsomely adjusted by double bust darts, narrow underarm gores, side-back seams and a center seam that terminates at the top of an underfolded box-plait below the waistline. The side-back seams are terminated at a similar point and an extension left on each front edge of the back skirt is unfolded in a backward-turning plait. The basque shapes a deep point in front, is short over the hips and falls in a square position at the back. It is made of the Jersey cloth; its high standing collar is covered by a row of braid like that decorating the drapery. Buttons and buttonholes close the front and three buttons are placed in a line on the wrist in front of the outside seam of the coat sleeve.

A costume of this kind may be evolved from any two varieties of dress goods or may be fashionably made from two colors in one texture. Velvet, plain, embroidered or brocaded is used with fabrics of all kinds. Very often the contrasting goods is seen only in the bodice of basque. Any garniture preferred may be added to the skirt; however, flat garnitures are most stylish on the draperies. The panel may be of the contrasting goods or may be elaborately ornamented, as preferred.

The felt hat is stylishly trimmed with braid like that decorating the costume, and handsome plumage.

LADIES' COSTUME.

9667
Right Side-Front View.

9667
Left Side-Back View.

LADIES' COSTUME.

9808
Front View.

9808
Side-Back View.

1885
Ladies' Costume

No. 9808. — The present illustration shows a combination of heavy Surah and fine novelty suiting. The skirt is of the Surah and has a side-plaiting of the same about six inches deep for its edge garniture, the plaiting being set on to form its own heading. It is of fashionable width and hangs gracefully; upon its gores are arranged at each side two long panels that fall even with the edge of the skirt. The front panels flare prettily toward the sides of the front-gore and are widely overlapped by the broader panels, which extend from the side-back seams. Drooping quite low over the center of the front-gore is a *tablier*-drapery, that crosses the panels and is draped very high on the hips by plaits in the top and sides, the plaits cross-wrinkling it handsomely. Three rows of narrow tinsel braid are applied to the edge of the *tablier*, also to the front and lower edges of the

panels, the inner row on the panels being coiled in a single loop at the corners. The back-drapery is plainly finished at its edges, falls almost to the edge of the skirt and is draped high and puffy by plaits clustered high up in its front edges and loopings to the skirt at the center.

The body of the costume is strikingly novel in effect. It has a handsome vest that is closed all the way down with buttonholes and buttons, pointed at the end of the closing and closely adjusted by double bust darts and narrow underarm gores. Overhanging the vest are jaunty jacket-fronts that roll back in broad lapels to a little below the bust and are cut away below. The jacket fronts are shorter than the vest, thus exposing the vest between and below them most attractively. Single bust darts and narrow underarm gores smoothly fit the jacket fronts, which are lined with the Surah, the lining being attractively exhibited by the lapels. The lower edges of the jacket fronts

and the front edges below the lapels are bordered with two rows of braid, the inner row being coiled at the lower front corner to correspond with the disposal on the panels. The three seams of the back terminate at the waistline at the top of underfolded double box-plaits, which flare handsomely over the *tournure*. A high standing collar encircles the neck and is concealed at the back by a high rolling collar that extends no further forward than the tops of the lapels and heightens attractively the jaunty air of the costume. About the wrists of the coat sleeves are two rows of the braid, the upper row being coiled in fancy design near the outside seam. A ruff of thin muslin is worn in the neck.

The fancy straw hat is prettily trimmed with double cords about the crown and a long-looped bow of ribbon in front. Its brim is smoothly faced with velvet, edged with a row of cord.

1885
Ladies' Costume

No. 9797. — This costume is an exhibition of one of the most stylish and exquisite modes for cotton and sheer goods of all kinds. It is here developed in Kursheedt's plain Chambray, with Kursheedt's embroidered Chambray trimming in two widths for garniture. The skirt is fashioned in the prevailing round walking style and has upon it at the right side a short, much-wrinkled drapery that is widely overlapped by the left drapery, which falls almost to the foot of the skirt and slants gracefully backward. This deep drapery crosses to the right hip at the top, but its lower front corner comes to the left of the center of the front. Two deep plaits laid high up in its back edge drape it handsomely. The right drapery is draped by gathers in its front and back edges and a row of the narrow embroidery turns upward from its lower edge. A row of the wide embroidery turns over flatly from the slanting front edge of the left drapery, with handsome effect. A narrow knife-plaiting forms the foot trimming for the skirt; above it the portion of the gores not concealed by the draperies are covered by three flounces of the deep embroidery, the lower flounce being continued across the back-breadth.

The deep, square back-drapery is provided by the over-dress, which is in basque style at the front and sides and closely fitted by double bust darts, narrow under-arm gores, side-back seams and a center seam, the latter three seams terminating in extra widths below the waistline. The center extra width is draped in bow fashion on the outside by a tape run in a casing formed underneath at the center and extending some distance below the top, the top of the drapery being caught to the body with a hook and loop. Plaits in the side edges complete the *bouffant* draping of the back, the side edges of which are hemmed for some distance from the lower edge and left loose. Buttons and buttonholes close the front, which is pointed at the end of the closing; at each side of the closing is a forward-turning row of the narrow embroidery applied in vest outline and graduated narrower above and below the bust. The embroidery is continued above the lower part of the basque portion with elaborate effect; a row of it turns upward in cuff fashion from the wrists of the coat sleeves. The high standing collar is covered with a row of the narrow embroidery turning upward from the seam.

The straw hat has its rolling brim smoothly faced with velvet. It is stylishly trimmed with a wide band of velvet arranged about the crown and a bunch of handsome ostrich plumage.

LADIES' COSTUME.

9797
Right Side-Front View.

9797
Left Side-Back View.

1885
Misses' Costume

No. 9771. — Very picturesque and novel is this costume, which is here developed in figured sateen, the girdle being made of velvet. The skirt is of the required depth and of the four-gored shape, and is trimmed at the bottom with a gathered ruffle of the material finished to form a self-heading and bordered at the lower edge with a row of lace. The front-drapery is deep and oval and has three forward-turning plaits at each side of the center at its top. It is also draped by deep plaits in its side edges, all the plaits contributing to its gracefully draped effect. A frill of lace edges the drapery; just above it is another ruffle turned down over its seaming. The back-drapery is also oval in outline and is very puffy in its draping, the result of deep plaits in its side edges and a looping at the center. It is gathered at the top and its loose edges are bordered with a frill of lace.

The waist is in Spencer style, smoothly fitted across the shoulders and gathered twice at the bottom at each side of the closing of the fronts and also at the center of the back. Side and shoulder seams shape it suitably, the adjustment being smooth under the arms. The standing collar is covered by a frill of lace falling over from its top, the lace being continued in cascade style down the closing to a little below the bust. A rosette of ribbon is fastened to the collar a little to the left of the closing. The waist is finished with a belt to which is also joined the skirt. The coat sleeves fit nicely and are trimmed with a ruffle of lace headed by a ruffle of narrower width.

The girdle is deeply pointed at the top and bottom at the center of the front and back, where it is laced with silk cord. It is lined with silk and has bones inserted in casings formed in the lining at each side of the lacings. At the sides it is quite shallow, but is curved to fit the figure smoothly. Although velvet is the material most frequently selected for such accessories, any other material preferred may be chosen, with good results.

For sheer goods, also for sateen and cotton goods of all kinds, the costume is very pretty and stylish; laces and embroideries will be lavishly used as garnitures. Summer silks, nun's-vailings and cashmeres in plain and figured varieties and all sorts of plain and figured suitings are adapted to costumes of this style, with braids, laces, embroideries, etc., for trimming. When the material chosen for the girdle warrants the application of garnitures, it will sometimes be elaborately beaded or embroidered.

This costume is suitably developed for misses from eight to fifteen years of age.

MISSES' COSTUME.

9771
Back View.

9771
Front View.

1885 Misses' Polonaise

No. 9655. — Plain cashmere and striped silk are united in the construction of this polonaise at Misses' Figure No. 5.

In the composition of the garment special care has been exercised to produce a picturesque effect without rendering the mode too elaborate for youthful wearers. The material chosen for it in the present instances is plain dress goods; the decorations consist of ribbon and Kursheedt's Standard striped tinsel braid. In the process of fitting single bust and underarm darts, side-back seams and a center seam are introduced. The three back seams are terminated a little below the waistline, the fullness below them being underfolded to form two box-plaits on the outside, these plaits being double at their inner and single at their outer folds. The back falls in a deep, square outline and has four upturning plaits folded in each side just below the hip, and the *bouffant* effect so fashionable is attained by forming some of the length in a loose, inward-falling loop and tacking it at the end of each side-back seam. Tapes fastened at the ends of the side-back seams and also at the center seam and at their opposite ends to the drapery lower down contribute to the effect, the center tape being also tacked once between its ends to the drapery. The closing of the front is invisibly accomplished by means of hooks and loops, the right side being hemmed and the left underfaced; below the closing the drapery is rounded off in graceful curves toward the back edges. In each front edge below the closing three upturning plaits are folded so that they overlap each other. At each back edge the same number, separated by short spaces, are also folded, this arrangement giving the *panier* effect so generally becoming and so very improving to many figures. The plaited front edges are seamed together; beneath the *paniers* are adjusted the deep front-drapery sections, which fall with entire plainness and lap, one upon the other, at their upper corners, below which their front edges separate in a broad flare. Their tops are conformed to the hips by a short dart in each and are sewed flatly underneath to the fronts, the back edges being sewed to the adjoining edges of the back-drapery and the *panier* portions included in the seams. Strips of braid are arranged horizontally at each side of the closing, their lengths being graduated slightly shorter toward the waistline and their back ends turned under to form points. The same arrangement of trimming is visible upon the front edges of the deep front-drapery, and over the plaits in the front edges of the *paniers* a handsomely looped bow of ribbon is tacked. The final

9655
Front View.

9655
Back View.

Figure No. 5. — MISSES' POLONAISE COSTUME.

arrangement of the draperies is perfected by means of tapes sewed beneath the side seams and tied together to hold the fronts as closely to the figure as is desirable and keep the back within a fashionably narrow limit. The sleeves are in coat shape and are prettily trimmed at the wrists with pointed strips of braid arranged perpendicularly and graduated so that their length increases regularly toward the outside of the arm. A high standing collar finishes the neck.

Two materials will often be united in a polonaise of this style, the contrasting fabric being used for the deep front-draperies, for cuff facings and for the collar. A polonaise showing a tasteful combination has the part specified of plaid goods showing red and dark blue, and the remainder of dark blue serge. The skirt to be worn with it is of the plain goods with a tiny plaiting of the same headed by a bias band of plaid for trimming. All kinds of braids, velvet ribbons, feather bands, etc., may be applied to such over-dresses; but over-elaboration in the application of trimming is not in good taste.

This pattern is suitable for misses from eight to fifteen years of age.

MISSES' COSTUME.

9773
Front View.

9773
Back View.

1885
Misses' Costume

This illustrates a Misses' costume. No. 9773. — This is a very charming costume for promenading or traveling, and is here made of light twilled cloth and trimmed with Kursheedt Standard tinsel braid. The skirt is gathered all round at the top, most of the fullness being, however, pushed well to the back and comprises only two sections which are of such dimensions and are requisite to contribute the fashionable width to the garment. A deep hem and five deep tucks are made in the skirt and the sewing of the tucks may be visible or invisible, as preferred. The *tablier*-drapery is very short and is softly wrinkled by plaits in its side edges. The back-drapery is deep and oval, and is full and puffy in its draping, which is made by plaits high up in the side edges. Two rows of tinsel braid trim the lower part of the *tablier*.

The basque is given a very jaunty air by a belt of leather buckled about the waist. It is close-fitting, the adjustment being made by single bust darts, underarm gores, and center and side-back seams that terminate at the top of underfolded box-plaits below the waistline. It is uniform in depth all round, and is trimmed in harmony with the *tablier* with two rows of tinsel braid. The coat sleeves are trimmed at the wrists to correspond, and a row of the braid overlies the standing collar. Buttons and buttonholes close the front.

For light-weight cloths and flannels, also for Cheviot suitings, serges, cashmeres, bourettes, etc., this will be a much-favored fashion; braid will be frequently selected as a garniture. The mode is also stylish and suitable for linens, seersuckers, cambrics, ginghams, sateens and white goods and dress fabrics of all varieties. Lace or embroidery may be added to the drapery edges and to the basque with very dainty results.

This costume is suitably developed in Pattern No. 9773 for misses from eight to fifteen years of age.

The straw bonnet has a puffing of velvet on its edge, and a full-looped bow of wide ribbon trims it. Ribbon ties are bowed stiffly beneath the chin.

1885 Girls' Sailor Costume

No. 9777. — In this instance the costume is developed in dark green flannel wth crimson flannel for the sailor collar, the cuff facings and the deep band on the skirt; dark green braid is very effectively arranged on the bright color. The skirt is full and is deeply shirred at the top and joined to a low-necked, sleeveless waist of lining goods. The waist is nicely shaped by side and shoulder seams and buttons in front. At the bottom of the skirt is applied a deep band of the crimson flannel that is even with the lower edge and is decorated more than half-way below the top with lines of braid.

The blouse is shaped by side and shoulder seams and buttons in front. It is high in the neck and is drawn in at the waist by an elastic cord or band inserted in the facing finishing the lower edge, the blouse being sufficiently long to droop in the required manner. At the neck is a little standing collar and a deep sailor-collar that extends to the bust in tapering lapels. The sailor collar is bordered with four lines of braid. The sleeves are in the comfortable coat style and are trimmed with deep cuff-facings of the bright flannel decorated at the top with three lines of braid.

Such costumes are always favored for little women, not only for their pictur-esqueness and jaunty appearance but also for their comfortable adjustment. Flannels, cashmeres, serges, vigognes and soft woolens are the favorite materials for them with braids, fancy stitchings done with floss or silk, machine-stitching or contrasting bands or facings for their completion. Ginghams, seersuckers, prints, piqués, sateens, cotton foulards and Ottomans, etc., will be much used for such costumes during the coming season, and the decorations will be similar to those on woolens. Lace or embroidery applied in flat rows will also decorate them.

Pattern No. 9777 is suitable for girls from five to twelve years of age.

GIRLS' SAILOR COSTUME.

9777
Front View.

9777
Back View.

GIRLS' COSTUME. Pattern No. 9663.

Front View.

Back View.

1885
Girls' Costume

No. 9663. — The union of three materials in the present instance is productive of a very attractive result. The skirt is of plaid goods showing a dark ground crossed by intersecting bars of two colors and is formed of straight breadths jointed together, turned under for a wide hem at the lower edge, laid in broad side-plaits all turning one way and sewed at the top to a shallow, fitted yoke, the ends extended by a slash made between the fold of the plait at the center of the back. A belt finishes the top of the yoke. A good pressing done on the under side is all that is needed to hold the plaits in position.

The body of the costume is a stylish jacket that has under or vest fronts of Ottoman silk which close with buttonholes and buttons, the right side being hemmed and the left underfaced; below the closing

they are cut away in a shallow point at each side. The outer or fronts proper are cut away from the tops of the shoulder seams nearly to the end of the vest closing and then are slanted off backward, leaving quite a broad flare between them. There is an underarm dart in each jacket front; in this dart seam is included the back edge of the vest portion, while the shoulder edge is sewed with the jacket portion to the back. The latter is fitted by side-back seams and a center seam, all three of which, and also the side seams, terminate below the waistline, leaving each section of the back to fall in a long, narrow tab, the effect being very ornamental. The sleeves are in coat shape and each is ornamented with three buttons placed upon the upper side in front of the outside seam. There is a high standing collar of Ottoman about the neck; in the same seam with it at the back is sewed a deep sailor-collar which, like the jacket proper, is of velvet. In front of the shoulder seams this collar is extended in

long, tapering ends which join the front edge of the jacket portion as far as the point of closing, which is accomplished with a single buttonhole and button.

The combination of fabrics may be limited to two kinds, or the costume may be developed in one material throughout. The triple combination is, however, much liked and will often be followed. When one material is preferred, the vest and the wrists of the sleeves will be ornamented with braid, lace, etc. The kilt is, in itself, so pretty that trimming is rarely added, though flat garnitures of any kind may be applied before the plaits are laid, if desired. An attractive costume unites Mazarin-blue velvet and mode-and-blue striped Ottoman. The kilt is arranged so that the lighter color is only made visible by the movements of the wearer; and the vest is of chamois.

Very appropriate for girls from five to twelve years of age is Pattern No. 9663.

1885
Girls' Costume

The costume will be one of the most popular styles during the coming season for little women, and is quaint and very picturesque in appearance. It is here very richly developed in cashmere, velvet and India muslin, with the sash-ties of ribbon; the fancy stitching is done with crimson silk. The *guimpe* is of the India muslin which is tucked uniformly for the front and back. Side and shoulder seams shape the *guimpe* nicely and buttonholes and buttons perform the closing at the back. A ruff of lace affords a dainty finish at the neck. The sleeves, which fit smoothly at the top, are gathered at the wrists to narrow bands that are wide enough to permit the hands to pass through easily, and are finished with a frill of the muslin.

The waist is of velvet and suggests the picturesque peasant style. It has short shoulder seams, the back being slightly low in the neck. The fronts open widely over the *guimpe* and are held together by four straps that are sewed to the right front and buttoned to the left front, the lowest strap being even with the lower edges and the upper one crossing at the bust. The left ends of the straps are pointed and two buttons corresponding with those fastening each are sewed just back of the other ends. Fancy stitching done with embroidery silk decorates the neck and front edges of the waist. Side-gores and a center seam fit the waist smoothly, and to the lower edges of the waist and lowest strap is joined the full skirt which is gathered all around at the top. A deep hem finishes the bottom of the skirt; above it are three moderately deep tucks. A row of fancy stitching like that decorating the waist is made above the upper tuck. In the underarm seams of the waist just above the skirt are inserted the plaited ends of wide sash-ties, and these are handsomely bowed at the center of the back.

Fancy stitching done with embroidery floss or silk or with crewels is much admired on costumes for little women and may be like the material in color of in decided contrast, as preferred. The waist, skirt and ties may all be of one material, and only the *guimpe* need be in contrast if desired, with pretty results. Lace or plain tucking, lace net, embroidered webbing or plain nainsook, lawn, etc., may be chosen for the *guimpe*. Cashmere, nun's-vailing or any light woolen suiting, and also chambray, linen, nainsook, plain and colored lawns, etc., may be selected for such dresses; the *guimpe* will usually be white, as the most picturesque result is produced with the spotless fabric. Of course,

GIRLS' COSTUME.

9769
Front View.

9769
Back View.

when the visible portion is of an ornamental material, all the concealed portions may be of plain goods.

Girls from three to twelve years of age can wear this pattern.

CHILD'S COSTUME.

9786
Front View.

9786
Back View.

1885
Child's Costume

No. 9786. — In this instance the costume is made of Kursheedt's plain Chambray and trimmed with Kursheedt's Standard embroidered Chambray edging and facings of tucked nainsook. The costume comprises a dress and over-dress, both permanently attached. The dress is shaped to cling gracefully to the figure by side and shoulder seams and closes at the back. The over-dress is cut low and square at the neck and has three box-plaits folded in it at the back and front, the plaits being sewed to position along their under-folds for some distance below the

neck. A frill of embroidery turns over from the square neck, above which the dress is covered with the white nainsook tucked uniformly, the material being cut away beneath, thus giving suggestions of a *guimpe*. Below the waistline the over-dress is shirred all round and sewed through the shirring to the dress so that it droops in a picturesque fashion over the shirring. A ruffle of the embroidery trims the bottom of the skirt and blouse, the material being cut away from underneath, thus producing a pretty effect. A row of embroidery turns upward in fancy cuff fashion from the wrists of the sleeves.

All varieties of white and figured cotton goods, also nun's-vailings, cashmeres and

light-textured woolens in plain and embroidered varieties, are handsome made up into costumes of this style; the yoke-like facing will usually be of lace or embroidered net, lace or plain tucking, plaited or shirred Surah or a contrasting color or fabric. Laces, embroideries, braids, plaitings, ruffles, or fancy stitching done with silk flosses or crewels, will be the usual trimming.

The child's costume, Pattern No. 9786, is suitable for children from two to six years of age.

The straw hat is prettily trimmed with ribbon.

1885
Child's Dress

No. 9658. — Very simple, yet very pretty is this little dress, which is here made of plain gingham. The body is long and loose fitting. It closes at the back with buttonholes and buttons and has only underarm and shoulder shaping seams. To its lower edge is joined a short skirt that is gathered all round at the top and surmounted by a ruffle of the material set on to form its own heading. The skirt is bordered near the lower edge with three rows of braid, and the ruffle with two rows. A tiny standing ruffle of the material and a deeper falling ruffle, separated by a very narrow band, complete the neck; the deeper ruffle is bordered with two rows of braid. Three rows of braid encircle the wrists of the coat sleeves.

Such dresses may be made of white, colored, printed, plaid and plain goods, and are especially simple and pretty for wash goods. The skirt may be of embroidered flouncing and the ruffles of embroidery when a dressy garment is desired. Beautiful little dresses of this style have the body of lace net or embroidered webbing and the ruffles and skirt of lace or embroidery.

This dress is suitable for children from two to six years of age.

CHILD'S DRESS.

9658
Front View.

9658
Back View.

1885
Girls' Costume

No. 9779. — This costume is handsomely illustrated in a combination of nun's-vailing and Surah, with lace for trimming, at Girls' Figure No. 6.

Cashmere and silk are united in the development of the costume in the present instance, and the effect of the combination is especially attractive. The body is fashionably long-waisted and is adjusted by seams upon the shoulders side seams placed well back and underarm darts, the latter being also taken through jacket-like portions almost meet at the throat and flare broadly below, revealing a vest of silk which is shirred twice at the throat and once at its lower edge and sewed flatly at its sides upon the body proper. The back edges are curved, finished with underfacings and closed with button-holes and buttons; to the lower edge is joined the skirt, which is formed of straight breadths joined together, turned under for a hem at the bottom and laid in box-plaits. The joining is concealed by a sash formed of three sections of silk, one of which is shirred at its center and plaited at each end. It is sewed through the shirring upon the center plait of the front, and its ends are tacked at the back and concealed by the sash-bow, which is in one piece and is plaited and tacked to form two loops and short, floating ends. The tackings and plaits of the bow are concealed by the third section which is simply a little cross-piece. The sleeves are in coat shape; each is ornamented at the wrist with three rows of narrow tinsel braid. Three rows of braid are arranged upon the front edges of the jacket fronts and about the skirt above the hem.

Plain and plaid Surah and wool goods will be made up in this way, and so will plain and embroidered chambrays, nun's-vailings, etc. One material may be used throughout, but scarcely with as good effect as when a combination is developed. Lace, embroidered edging or any decoration preferred may be added. Sometimes the vest will be omitted and the front between the jacket edges will be overlaid with ruffles of lace or embroidery, or it may be ornamented with braid arranged in some tasteful fashion.

Pattern No. 9779 is desirable for the wardrobe of a girl three to nine years of age.

Figure No. 6. — GIRLS' COSTUME.

9779
Front View.

9779
Back View.

1885
Girls' Costume

No. 9708. — Girls' figure No. 9.

Dress goods having a plain, soft finish and Surah silk are represented in the present instance; the effect is particularly attractive. The skirt is composed of three gores for the front and sides and a full breadth for the back; the gores are fitted smoothly while the breadth is gathered into the proper size at each side of the placket opening. A fine side-plaiting, set on to form its own heading, trims the lower edge, and the top is sewed to a waist that extends a fashionable depth below the hips and has seams upon the shoulders and at the sides, its back edges being curved out to assist in the adjustment, finished with underfacings and closed with buttonholes and buttons. Upon the front is adjusted a Moliére vest of Surah which is appropriately curved out at the neck and gathered twice to within a short distance of the shoulder edges, the latter being included in the shoulder seams and the neck edge finished, with the neck of the waist, by a narrow bias binding. The lower edge is gathered and sewed with the waist to the skirt, and the extra length of the vest falls in a little loop at each side below concealed by the fronts of the over-dress. A sash piece of the goods with its ends, which are each shirred up, extending upward upon the body a little at the side seams, where they are sewed flatly. The top is turned in and tacked at its center over the skirt seam and once between this tacking and each end to the body portion. The over-dress is in polonaise fashion; the fronts meet at the throat and flare below, disclosing the vest and forming a decided point low down at each side. There is an underarm dart in each side of the front. At the center of the back is a curving seam which completes the adjustment in the regular French fashion. The center seam terminates a little below the waistline, and the drapery is widened sufficiently below it to permit of being very prettily arranged. It is turned in quite deeply for a finish at the top, and at the center four upward-turning plaits are tacked. The top is tacked to position a little above the end of the center seam, and the result is to draw the drapery up with a double-pointed sash effect. Lace is sewed beneath the front and lower edges of the front-draperies and turned backward and upward flatly upon the outside. Lace also trims the wrists of the coat shaped sleeves, and is sewed flatly upon the high rolling collar.

As decided or dainty a contrast as may be admired may be developed in the construction of a costume of this style. One charming example of the mode has the vest and the sash-piece of cherry-colored Surah and the remainder of the toilette of gray cashmere. Another, of white flannel throughout, has the portions trimmed with lace in the present instance and bordered with several rows of narrow soutache braid.

Girls from five to twelve years of age will look attractive in Pattern No. 9708.

9708
Front View.

No. 9. — GIRLS' COSTUME. —
No. 9708. — Girls' Figure No. 9.

9708
Back View.

1885
Child's Dress

No. 9780. — This dress is developed in fancy suiting, with collar and cuff-facings of silk, at Child's Figure No. 5.

A simpler and yet a more attractive style of dress could scarcely be pictured. Cambric is the material illustrated in the present instance and embroidery forms the trimming. The front is cut on a fold of the goods and has six tucks turning toward the center stitched in it from the neck and shoulders to within a short distance of the lower edge; turning toward the closing edges of the back are six similar tucks. Both sides of the back are hemmed and the closing is made with buttonholes and buttons. The side seams are sprung out toward the lower edge and this provision, in conjunction with the width released below the stitchings of the tucks, gives all the fullness required about the bottom of the dress. Embroidery is applied with slight fullness upon the lower edge and also about the wrists of the little coat sleeves. At the neck is a wide, flat collar in two sections, the corresponding ends flaring at the center of the front and back. Wide embroidery finishes the edges of the collar, and in the same seam with the narrow binding which is about the neck is sewed a standing ruffle of the narrower variety. About the waist is worn a sash formed of a wide strip of the goods, which is drawn in loose wrinkles about the figure and tied in a large bow at the back.

Lawn, gingham, chambray, print, cashmere, Surah and all materials vogue for children's dresses make up tastefully in this way. The sash may be of ribbon or it may be omitted altogether if not desired, the costume being complete without it. Lace in pressed Italian, Fedora and oriental varieties may be chosen for trimming when the texture of the goods invites such decorations. Colored embroideries are this season more popular than ever before.

Pattern No. 9780 will make up attractively for children from one to six years of age.

9780
Front View.

9780
Back View.

Figure No. 5. — CHILD'S DRESS.

1885
Child's Dress

No. 9823. — A tasteful illustration of this dress is given at Child's Figure No. 3, where it is developed in cashmere, with heavy lace and buttons for its decorations.

Piqué is the material represented in the present instance and Hamburg edging and insertion form the trimming. The body is fashionably long-waisted and has seams upon the shoulders and at the sides. In each side of the back and at each side of the center of the front a box-plait is stitched in its folds for the entire depth, and between and back of these plaits bands of insertion are stitched with very ornamental effect, that between the plaits in the back being, of course, applied only on the overlapping side; the closing is invisibly accomplished by button-holes and small buttons. To the lower edge is sewed the skirt, which is short in proportion to the depth of the body and is formed of straight breadths joined together, turned under for a hem at its lower edge, turned in for a finish at the top and laid in medium-wide box-plaits. The skirt is sewed to the body far enough from the top to form its own heading; its ornamental effect is enhanced by the application of a row of insertion above the hem before the plaits are laid. The sleeves are in coat shape and are long enough to extend to the wrists, but in this instance they are slightly shortened to permit of the addition of frills of embroidery at their lower edges, that decorations being surmounted by bands of insertion. There is a narrow bias binding about the neck; inside it is sewed a full frill of embroidery. Plain and embroidered chambrays will be much liked for dresses of this description, either singly or in combination. Embroidered flouncing deep enough to cut the skirt from is easily procured in all colors and in many varieties of goods and, being very ornamental, is much admired for best frocks. Simpler decorations are, however, in just as good taste, and for general wear are more durable and satisfactory.

Pattern No. 9823 has been designed for children from one to six years of age.

Figure No. 3. — CHILD'S DRESS. — This illustrates Pattern No. 9823.

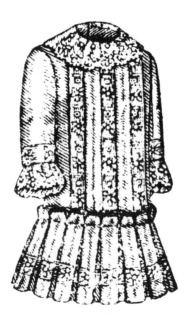

9823
Front View.

9823
Back View.

Back.

Front.

1886
Girls' Polonaise

It is the purpose of this department, as all our old subscribers know, to give the latest fashion of its kind: a polonaise, jacket, mantle, waist, cloak or some other article of dress. Whoever takes "Peterson," therefore, will be sure to get, every month, not only a score of costumes to select from, but also the very latest and most stylish article out, with a dress pattern of it: which, if made up, will put the wearer ahead of all others in fashion.

For this month, we give a Girl's Polonaise. The engraving annexed shows how this polonaise looks when made up.

1886
Ladies' Costume

We give the front and back view of this costume. The material used may be either figured or plain and the model is suitable for China silks, embroidered étamines — in fact, any of the more dressy thin goods for summer wear. The skirt has a narrow knife-plaited ruffle as edge above which, on the front-breadth, are seven lace or embroidered flounces. Our model calls for torchon lace. The over-drapery is a simple plain skirt all around, hemmed on the edge. It hangs straight on the left side. The right side is looped, as seen in the illustration, which also shows, in the back view, how it is plaited in at the waist. The bretelle-front of the bodice is made entirely of the lace, laid on flat, and adjusted to form a narrow point at the waist. Standing collar and cuffs, to match.

1886 Ladies' Everyday Costume

This is a costume of washing-material
—striped gingham, seersucker or étamine.
The latter is a new fabric; looks like lace
muslin, with embroidered pin-stripes; comes
in écru with brown; also écru with brown
and blue or red in the stripes, with embroidery to match. This model is very simple,
easily made and requires no trimming, being
composed entirely of the material. The
material is used crosswise for the three deep
flounces which compose the entire skirt.
These flounces may be either gathered or
kilt-plaited; the latter is more elegant and
stylish. The foundation-skirt, which is of the
same material, is made lengthwise. The
bodice, sleeves and short flounce, which
trims the edge of the pointed bodice, all
lengthwise of the material. The ribbons or
sash, of the same, begin from the side-seams
of the bodice. The back of the bodice may be
finished in a short point, to match the front
or a box-plaited postillion. The collar is tied
to match the sash at the waist. A tiny capote
of the material completes this costume. This
model will serve equally well for any of the
light woolen textures — such as nun's-
veiling, albatross, crêpe-cloth, etc. — but
not for the rough goods. They must be made
with plain skirts and long clinging drapery.

1886 Ladies' Dresses

WALKING DRESS. GARDEN PARTY DRESS.

1886 Ladies' Dresses

WALKING DRESS. VISITING DRESS.

LES MODES PARISIENNES: PETERSON'S MAGAZINE.
JUNE, 1886. A SUMMER AFTERNOON.

1886
Ladies' Bodice

This is a new bodice for spring and summer wear made of lightweight lady's cloth. This model is of crimson cloth, braided with black worsted braid, in military style, as seen in the illustration. The bodice has a postillion-back. The braid is put on the sleeves to simulate a deep cuff. High standing collar, braided to match.

These stylish red jackets will be extremely fashionable for mountain and seaside wear, for cool mornings and for driving.

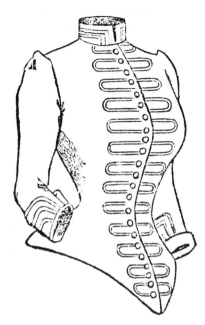

Bodice.

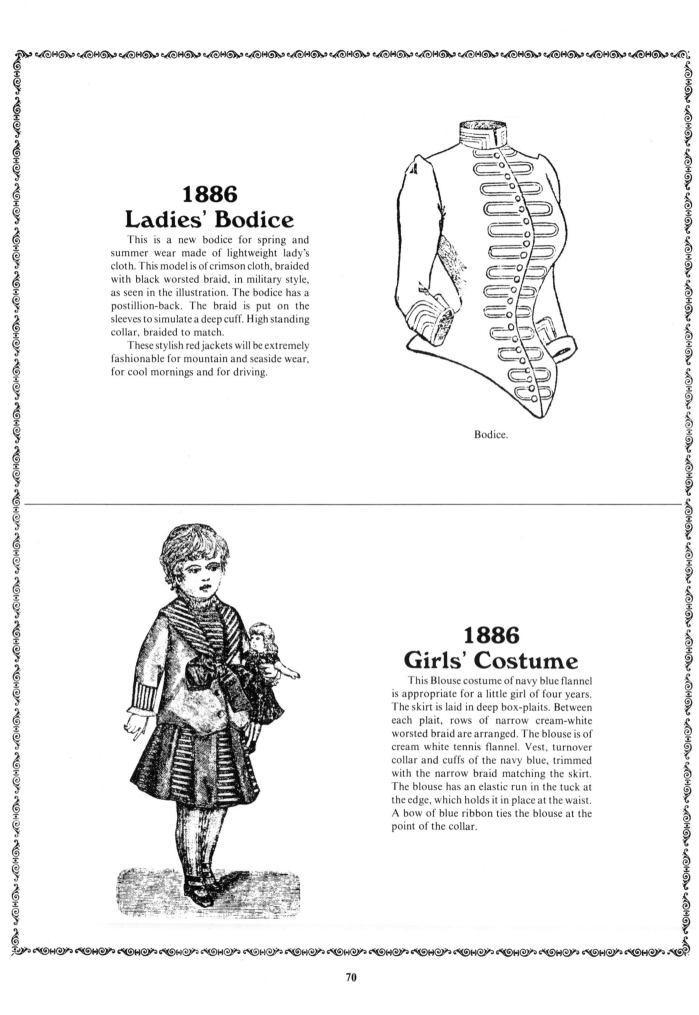

1886
Girls' Costume

This Blouse costume of navy blue flannel is appropriate for a little girl of four years. The skirt is laid in deep box-plaits. Between each plait, rows of narrow cream-white worsted braid are arranged. The blouse is of cream white tennis flannel. Vest, turnover collar and cuffs of the navy blue, trimmed with the narrow braid matching the skirt. The blouse has an elastic run in the tuck at the edge, which holds it in place at the waist. A bow of blue ribbon ties the blouse at the point of the collar.

1886
Girls' Dress

For a girl of eight years or so, we have a walking costume of mixed light summer woolens. Our model is of bronze-green. The skirt is kilt-plaited of plain, as the taste may decide. The long jacket-bodice is simply trimmed with one row of olive-wood beads; the collar, cuffs, and pockets likewise. Waistcoat of écru embroidery.

1887
Ladies' Costume

No. 1518. — This consists of a Ladies' skirt and polonaise.

In this instance plain and embroidered nun's-vailing are associated in the costume. The skirt is the popular round style and is plainly finished. It hangs evenly all round and is planned so that steels and a bustle may be worn or omitted, as desired.

The polonaise introduces a charming style of drapery and is fitted by double bust darts, underarm and side-back gores and a curving center seam. Its body is in basque style and its draperies are added. The front-draperies round away in graceful curves, flare decidedly and fall in an oval outline to a little below the knees. They are arranged in soft, irregular folds by gathers in the back edges, in the front edge of the left drapery and also across the top of the right drapery for some distance from the front edge. The right drapery is deepened nearly the width of

LADIES' POLONAISE COSTUME.

the gathers to extend to the neck with something of a full plastron effect; the extended portion is gathered at the neck and lies almost wholly on the right front, to which it is tacked down the back edge. The shirring at the bottom of the ornament is secured to a stay and has about it a long *moiré* ribbon that is tied in a bow with long loops and ends. Both draperies are tacked invisibly to the body at the top; the gathered front edge of the left drapery is also tacked to the body, but is concealed by the right drapery, which overlaps it prettily. The back-drapery is arranged alike at both sides and falls quite low on the skirt at the center, but is lifted quite high at the sides. It is gathered at the top and tacked to the body, and is also gathered for some distance at the sides where it joins the front-draperies, the seams being tacked to the body. Below the seams the edges are free and the drapery is tacked to a cross-strap so as to fall in folds that give the lower edge a pretty broken outline. An upright strap at the center and a tacking a little below the top at the center are useful in completing the handsome draping

of the back. A large bow of *moiré* ribbon is fastened over the top of each side seam in the drapery, with decorative effect. The ornament on the front conceals the closing. The collar is in the high standing style; the sleeves are in coat shape, being reversed at the wrists to form cuffs and faced with the plain material.

Instead of the embroidered material, striped figured, checked, plaid or mixed goods may be used if preferred, or any one of them may be used for the skirt and plain goods for the polonaise. Embroidered silks, cottons and woolens are, however, much the vogue, and the effect achieved with them is rich and handsome. Velvet, silk, Surah or *faille* may be used for the skirt when the polonaise is of wool goods or some sheer cotton fabric. For dressy wear China and India silks in plain and embroidered varieties will be handsome and summery looking, and so will nun's-vailings, batistes, *crêpes*, cashmeres and soft serges.

A facing of velvet covers the rolling brim of the straw hat, and a large *monture* of flowers and leaves affords the only trimming.

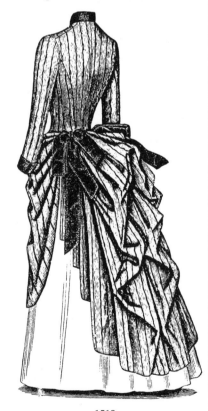

1518
Right Side-Front View.

1518
Left Side-Back View.

LADIES' COSTUME.

1887
Ladies' Costume

No. 1506. — The fashionable combination of velvet and cotton dress goods is here achieved in the costume, the cotton fabrics being plain and embroidered batiste. The skirt, being shaped in the popular four-gored style, hangs gracefully and may be worn with or without a bustle and steels. On either side of the gores are two flat panels that are finished with wide hems down their front edges and sewed to the skirt along the back of the hems, the panels farthest back overlapping the others the width of the hems. As the hems are sewed visibly the

1506
Side-Front View.

1506
Side-Back View.

effect of plaits is realized. The front-gore is of the embroidered goods and is revealed between the front panels, which are rendered decorative by a row of embroidered batiste edging applied to turn forward from beneath the hem of the overlapping panels. The panels fall even with the edge of the skirt and are smoothly fitted at the belt. The back-drapery is made *bouffant* over the bustle by two deep, downward-turning plaits in each side edge near the belt, and falls straight below even with the edge of the skirt.

A double-pointed vest of the embroidered goods is visible between the cutaway edges of the fronts, which flare toward the bottom and do not meet at the throat. Long lapels of velvet turn over the front edges of the fronts

all the way down and are broad above the bust and taper narrowly below. Three long buttonholes simulated with fine cord decorate the top of the lapels and, extending slightly above them on the basque, are terminated under three pretty buttons. The basque is adjusted by well curved darts and seams; the vest is sewed underneath to the fronts along the first bust darts and flatly above. The vest is closed invisibly with hooks and loops which are arranged to alternate on each side. The side seams terminate below the waistline; all the other seams are continued in their curves to the edge. To the lower edge of the front at either side is joined an ornament of velvet that is continued across the side nearly to the side

seams, turned up on the outside and caught like the top of the lapels to the basque with three simulated buttonholes of fine cord and three buttons. The ornaments are narrow at their tops and are tacked to place at their upper corners. The standing collar is of velvet and a bar-pin is fastened at its ends. A linen collar is also worn. The coat sleeves are trimmed at their wrists with deep, round cuffs of velvet, over which at the bottom turn shallow cuffs of the silk that flare at the back of the wrists. A button on the shallow cuffs and a simulated buttonhole of cord extending from it upon the velvet cuff complete the decoration in harmony with the other parts of the basque.

1887
Misses' Costume

No. 1509. — The admired *guimpe* and bodice effect is developed in this costume, which is here shown made of figured *challis* and plain silk, the silk being used for the bodice. A plain finish is observable at the edge of the skirt which is in the popular four-gored style. The draperies are prettily arranged and are deep and full. At the back the drapery falls even with the edge of the skirt and is made *bouffant* over the bustle by an effective arrangement of bournous loops, which is the only draping. The front-drapery is a deep, round *tablier* that falls in *jabot*-folds at the left edge, these folds being the result of carefully arranged plaits and tackings. Plaits at the belt and in the right side edge produce the soft folds characterizing the drapery. A facing of silk is disclosed by the *jabot*-folds and a decorative effect results from a frill of lace along the edges of the *jabot* and also along the remaining edges of the front drapery. A large sash-bow of wide ribbon is fastened over the top of the back-drapery at the right side and completes the appointments of the skirt.

The *guimpe* is fitted by side and shoulder seams; its upper part both back and front is covered with a puff-like yoke that is all in one piece and is gathered at the neck and lower edges. The sleeves are fitted smoothly into the arms'-eyes, but are gathered at their wrists to deep bands that are overlaid with a row of lace and made wide enough to slip easily over the hands. With the puff yoke the sleeves are exceedingly *chic*, and the effect of both is made pronounced by the tight-fitting bodice of silk. Like the *guimpe* the bodice is closed at the back, but its closing is made with cord laced through eyelets, while the *guimpe* is closed with buttonholes and buttons. A curving seam at the center of the front, underarm and side-back gores and single bust darts are used in the adjustment of the bodice, which is low enough to the neck to expose the puff yoke attractively, being lowest at the center of the front and at the closing. The front and back are held together on the shoulders by ribbons, which are plaited to their corners and tied in bows. The bodice outlines a deep point at the center of the front and back and a high arch over the hips. A standing collar is the approved finish for the *guimpe*; it is concealed by a frill of lace which falls over it from the top.

Oftentimes the *guimpe* will be of white sheer cotton or white China or India silk when the bodice is of velvet or silk and the skirt of plain or fancy wool goods. All sorts of picturesque combinations may be achieved in a costume of this style. *Challis* and nun's-vailings are much liked for misses'

MISSES' COSTUME.

1509
Left Side-Back View.

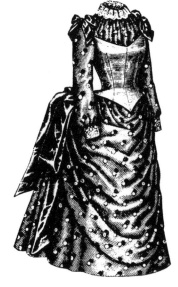

1509
Right Side-Front View.

costumes; they are frequently made up in combinations of plain and fancy varieties or with silk, Surah or velvet. This costume, Pattern No. 1509, was developed for eight to fifteen-years-olds.

1887
Misses' Costume

Figure No. 426. — This illustrates a Misses' costume.

The combination of blue and white is here developed, the material being Summer flannel. The skirt is in the four-gored shape and upon its gores, reaching nearly to the belt, is a flat drapery that is laid in wide box-plaits and hemmed at the bottom. A row of wide white braid is applied to the drapery above its hem and two narrower rows are arranged above, the three rows being carried across the back-breadth. The upper front-drapery is a *tablier* that is deeply reversed at its left side, the *revers* tapering to a point toward the center of the front and showing a smooth facing of the white flannel. It is effectively draped in cross-folds by plaits under the *revers* and in the right side edge. The back-drapery is lifted higher at the center than at the sides, drawing the lower edge into the approved "fish-tail" outline. A deep, loose loop in each side edge and graceful loopings done by plaits and tackings at the center develop a stylish *bouffant* effect over the bustle.

The body has jacket fronts that are turned over in small lapels at the throat, meet at the lower edges of the lapels and then flare in regular cutaway fashion over a shorter vest of the white flannel that is pointed at the center and closed with button-holes and ball-shaped buttons. The lapels are faced with the white flannel, and the vest is visible between them, while ties of blue ribbon secure the jacket fronts where they meet. The vest underlies the jacket fronts to the shoulder and back edges and bust darts fit both vest and jacket-fronts gracefully to the figure. At the back and sides the adjustment is close, underarm and side-back gores and a curving center seam producing the desired effect. The center seam ceases at the waistline; the edges below are hemmed and fall loosely. At the side-back seams a loose plait is formed on the outside below the waistline, and as the contour of the back is square, the effect of a position is rendered conspicuous by the pretty curve at the sides. The standing collar is of the blue goods; round cuffs of the white fabric trim the coat sleeves. White linen collar and cuffs are worn.

Pattern No. 1515 was designed for misses from eight to fifteen years of age.

The hat is a large shape in fancy straw and its brim is rolled on one side and smoothly faced with velvet; it is trimmed with velvet and ostrich plumage.

Figure No. 426. — MISSES' COSTUME. — This illustrates Pattern No. 1515.

1515
Right Side-Front View.

1515
Left Side-Back View.

1887 Girls' Garibaldi Costume

No. 1418. — Velvet and cashmere are charmingly associated in this costume at figure No. 377, ribbon forming the ties and bow and lacing cord and buttons adding to the daintiness of its decorations.

That the favor accorded the Garibaldi modes is not misplaced is amply proven by the pretty and practical qualities of the garments themselves. Soft gray serge was used for the costume here pictured. The back and front are each cut on a fold of the goods and the front has an opening extending from the throat nearly to the waistline. Yoke-shaped lining sections are provided for them, and upon these the outer portions are adjusted by shoulder shirrings, there being five rows made parallel with each shoulder edge both in the back and front; the first row in each group is close to the shoulder seam, the next nearly an inch from it, and the others about a quarter of an inch apart. All the shirrings are stayed by being sewed through to the lining sections; the fullness at the waistline is drawn in to the figure by means of a tape run through a casing sewed upon the under side, the ends being tied in front. The side seams are sprung out to assist in producing a becoming fullness about the lower part of the costume; the bottom is finished with a hem for which allowance is made in the pattern. At the left side of the opening in front is sewed a broad shield which extends half its width to the right of the opening. Upon the outside is applied a facing that is broadest at its top; the closing is made invisibly with hooks and loops. The collar is in the high rolling style. Each sleeve is formed of a single section of goods that is scantily gathered at the top and bottom, the gathers at the top being grouped at the upper side of the arm. The lower edge is sewed to a deep cuff or wristband, and over the joining of the wristband, a shallow, downward-turning plait is formed in each inner edge. These edges are then sewed together as far as the lower folds of the plaits. Hooks and eyes close the ends of the cuff. About the waist is worn a girdle of ribbon, which is bowed in front; at the throat is fastened a pretty bow of ribbon.

Sometimes the cuffs, collar and front facing will be of contrasting goods, or they will be trimmed with braid or velvet ribbon or overlaid with embroidery.

Pattern No. 1418 is for girls from three to nine years of age.

Figure No. 377. — GIRLS' GARIBALDI COSTUME.

1418
Back View.

1418
Front View.

GIRLS' DRESS AND *GUIMPE* (Blouse).

1514
Front View.

1514
Back View.
(To be worn with a *Guimpe.*)

1887 Girls' Dress and Guimpe

This consists of a girls' dress No. 1514 and *guimpe* No. 1526.

In this instance the dress is pictured as made of figured *challis*, and a pretty effect is achieved by the association of fine nainsook and colored embroidery in the *guimpe*, the embroidery showing the colors of the *challis*. The body of the dress is a short waist that has its neck cut in Pompadour shape both back and front and has side-plaits extending from the shoulders to the lower edge, both back and front. Between the plaits in the front the waist is plaited at the neck and gathered at the bottom; the same effect is produced in the back, down which the closing is made with buttonholes and buttons. At the sides the adjustment is smooth, and the fullness of the front and back is retained permanently in place by smooth-fitting lining portions which underlie these parts to the seams. The sleeves are in puff style and are gathered at the top and bottom and mounted on smooth lining portions that serve to retain their fullness in proper position. The skirt is hemmed at the bottom and has a broad double box-plait at either side of the center of the front; it is gathered back of the plaits and joined all round to the waist. A ribbon bow is fastened at the left side of the front with decorative effect. Above the square neck the embroidered material used for the upper part of the *guimpe* is visible; the high neck is finished with a binding of the white goods and a standing frill of white embroidery. The sleeves are in what is known as "shirt" style, and their deep wristbands are finished with frills of white embroidery that fall toward the hands. Side and shoulder seams shape the *guimpe* and a tape inserted in a casing regulates its adjustment about the waist.

White goods in plain or embroidered varieties will oftenest form the *guimpe*, but colored fabrics will frequently be used with original and picturesque results.

This costume is appropriate for girls from three to twelve years of age.

1887
Girls' Costumes

Figure No. 433. — Girls' Costume. —
The costume is here pictured as developed in cashmere, velvet, Surah and figured striped silk. The body and skirt are made separate and then seamed together. The fronts of the body open straight down over a full vest of Surah that is gathered at the neck and lower edges and mounted on a plain under-front of lining that fastens to a narrower front of lining down one side. These lining portions underlie the fronts to their back and shoulder edges. Over the top of the vest are arranged two ornamental, yoke-like sections of velvet that separate with a slight flare below the throat; they extend only a short distance below the throat, and tassel-tipped cord laced through eyelets holds their front edges together and produces a decorative effect. Underarm and side-back gores and a curving center seam make the adjustment. The skirt has two forward-turning plaits that flare at each side of the center of the front, and some distance back of these plaits it is laid in kilt-plaits that turn backward. The spaces between the two sets of plaits produce the effect of narrow panels which are made pronounced by a facing of the fancy silk. Girdle sections of velvet are laced together over and below the bottom of the vest, but do not extend quite to the underarm seams, their back ends being pointed and lapped over the plaited ends of wide sash-ties of silk that are arranged in an immense bow at the back. The cord is tipped with tassels and three buttons decorate the pointed ends. Deep cuffs of velvet that flare on the upper side of the wrists trim the coat sleeves and ruffs of lace are worn in the neck and sleeves.

If desired, only two materials need be combined in the costume; they may be of contrasting colors, varieties or textures.

Pattern No. 1545 is for girls from five to twelve years of age.

The wide-brimmed sailor-hat is of fancy straw, trimmed in the characteristic way with a band of ribbon and two short streamers.

Figure No. 432. — Girls' Dress.
Plain and embroidered chambray were here used for the dress and fine nainsook for the *guimpe*, the material being tucked for the upper part of the *guimpe*. Side and shoulder seams shape the *guimpe*; a tape inserted in a casing regulates width at the waist, buttons and buttonholes closing it at the back. The sleeves are in shirt style, being gathered at the bottom to bands that are wide enough to slip easily over the hands. Frills of white embroidery fall toward the hands from the bottom of the bands; a

Figures Nos. 432 and 433.
Figure No. 432. — GIRLS' DRESS. — This illustrates Pattern No. 1547.
Figure No. 433. — GIRLS' COSTUME. — This illustrates Pattern No. 1545.

similar frill stands at the neck outside the standing collar.

The dress has a pretty waist that is cut low in V shape both back and front. In the front a cluster of tucks is made at each side of the center; between the tucks the front shows the embroidered material. The tucks should be made before the waist is cut out and the embroidered goods inserted, as the front is perfectly plain and the present arrangement purely decorative. At the center of the front the waist is pointed at the lower edge, but at the sides and back it is round, a cording of the goods finishing the edge. A frill of the embroidered chambray edging turns over from the neck; similar frills trim the arms'-eyes. The skirt has at the center of the front a smooth gore which imparts a panel effect between the ends of the full portion forming the rest of it. The full portion is overhung more than half-way to the bottom by a flounce-drapery. Both it and the drapery are gathered at the top and joined to the edge of the waist. The gore also joins the edge of the waist except at the point, under which it is sewed flatly. The bottom of the gore is trimmed with a frill of wide embroidered chambray edging below a cluster of fine tucks; a frill of narrower

edging and a cluster of tucks trim the lower part of the drapery and the full portion of the skirt, the edging being carried from the bottom of the skirt up the side-front seams to the waist. A bow of ribbon having drooping loops and long ends is fastened over the top of the right seam, with dressy effect. Buttons and buttonholes close the waist at the back.

The simplicity of the construction will make the dress a popular fashion for all varieties of cotton textures. Soft woolens and Summer silks are also pretty when developed in this way, while cotton goods may be used for the *guimpe* no matter what texture is used for the dress, lawn, mull, net, embroidered webbing, nainsook and India muslin being especially nice for it. Flouncing may be used for the full part of the skirt, and also for the draping; if an elaborate effect be desired, the gore may be made of embroidered goods to match or be cross-trimmed with frills of edging.

This dress pattern was developed for girls from five to twelve years old.

The hat is a pretty shape in fancy yellow straw and has a smooth facing of velvet on its rolling brim. A bunch of flowers placed directly in front is the only trimming.

1545
Front View.

1545
Back View.

1547
Front View.

1547
Back View.

1887 Girls' Dress

No. 1507. — A simple and pretty style of dress for little women is this and it is here shown made of striped gingham. The body extends over the hips and is shaped to cling easily to the figure by underarm gores and curved back edges. To its lower edge is joined the full skirt, which is gathered all round the top and has a wide hem and three wide tucks made in it. Extending down either side of the front is a bias band of the material that forms a point below the body on the skirt and meets in the shoulder seam a similar band applied down either side of the back. The bands produce a bretelle-like decoration that is exceedingly becoming. The closing is made at the back and is concealed by a bias band like those just described. A bias standing collar finishes the neck and bias bands trim the coat sleeves, ruffs of lace being worn at the neck and wrists.

For such dresses all sorts of white and colored cottons, lawns, ginghams, nainsooks, muslins, etc., will be used, the simplicity of the mode rendering easy the task of laundering. Sometimes the body will be of embroidered goods and the skirt of embroidered flouncing, in which case the depth of the tucks and hem will be deducted from the pattern. Between the bands the front may be faced with contrasting goods. Serges, cashmeres and all sorts of soft woolens will also be thus made up, and so will Summer and other silks.

Pattern No. 1507 is suitable for girls from three to nine years of age.

The large straw hat is simply trimmed with ribbon.

GIRLS' DRESS.

1507
Back View.

1507
Front View.

1887
Girls' Costume

No. 1433. — The combination of fabrics here achieved renders the costume particularly rich and dressy cashmere, plain velvet and fancy-striped velvet being utilized. The fronts lap diagonally below the bust, above which they open in V shape to the shoulders over a vest of the required length that is inserted in Breton fashion. Underarm darts render the fronts clinging and smooth over the hips; to the lower edges of the fronts are joined the three gores forming the front and sides of the skirt. With these gores is also joined the top of the front-drapery, which forms a deep point at the left side and is rounding in outline from the end of the closing to the right side. Plaits clustered at the end of the closing and in both side edges wrinkle the drapery beautifully; a fancy ornament placed over the plaits at the closing appears to hold them in position, this suggestion of usefulness adding much to the value of the ornament. The back-drapery and back-breadth are finished at the top with a band that is caught underneath to the side seams, and over them the backs and side-backs fall in pretty tabs. Plaits at the center and plaits and bournous loops at the belt drape the back-drapery in two deep *bouffant* points that fall quite low upon the breadth. The neck is finished with a standing collar and a shawl collar is simulated with a facing of the striped velvet at the back and down the edges of the fronts. Cuff facings of plain velvet trim the coat sleeves prettily and ruffs are worn in the neck and wrists.

Less expensive fabrics may be similarly combined in such costumes and only two materials may be selected if preferred. One material may be used throughout with good effect, and the vest and skirt may be striped crosswise or lengthwise with braid or ribbon. Striped or plaid and plain or mixed goods are favored combinations for girls' costumes, and may be achieved with cotton, woolen or silken textures, many of the cotton textures having the same style of weaving as the wool goods. All kinds of dress goods are appropriate for a costume of this kind and any simple decoration may be added. The edges of the fronts may be trimmed with beads, flatly applied laces or embroideries, etc., or be plainly finished.

This costume has been developed for girls from five to twelve years old.

The pretty straw hat is simply trimmed with ribbon.

GIRLS' COSTUME. — Pattern No. 1433.

1433
Right Side-Front View.

1433
Left Side-Back View.

1887
Child's Dress

No. 1431. — Figured linen lawn and lace tucking are associated in this dress at Figure No. 382, and embroidery forming the trimming.

The selection of plain wash goods and embroidered webbing for the garment in the present instance indicates its suitability for the entire range of cotton textures for Summer wear. The body portion is fashionably long-waisted; its upper part is in yoke shape and has seams upon the shoulders. The full portion comprises three sections which are united by seams at the sides and are curved out above these seams to perfect the shape of the arm's-eye. The upper edges are turned in for a finish, and a row of shirring is made far enough from the top of each section to leave a little ruffled heading above it. The shirring extends nearly to the arm's-eye and through the headings the full portions are stitched upon the yoke. The right side of both the yoke and full portion are turned under for a hem; the closing is made with buttonholes and buttons. Gatherings terminating some distance front and back of the side seams adjust the lower edge of the waist to the proper size and are stayed to a tape or narrow strip placed underneath. To the lower edge of the body is joined the skirt, which is short in proportion to the length of the body and is formed of straight breadths joined together, turned under for a hem at the lower edge and gathered all round at the top. The joining is concealed by a belt of the goods, which closes at the left side of the front with three buttonholes and small buttons. The yoke is made of all-over embroidery, and the standing collar is ornamented with a ruffle of embroidered edging which is sewed outside and extends a little above it. The sleeves are in coat shape and are trimmed with embroidered edging which is turned back flatly from the wrists and arranged in a ruffle about each arm's-eye across the top of the sleeve.

The arrangement of the trimming about the arms'-eyes suggests the omission of the sleeves and also the development of the *guimpe* effect by making them and the yoke of material differing from the remainder of the dress. Very effective contrasts may be developed in this way.

Figure No. 382. — This illustrates a child's dress, Pattern No. 1431.

The combination here achieved shows figured linen lawn and Kursheedt's Standard lace tucking. The deep yoke forming the upper part of the dress at the back and front is of the tucking and so are the little coat sleeves. The neck is completed with a standing ruffle of embroidery and a ruffle of

Figure No. 382. — CHILD'S DRESS. — This illustrates Pattern No. 1431.

1431
Front View.

1431
Back View.

similar embroidery trims the wrists. The lower part of the body is full and *negligé*, and is shaped by side seams and gathered across the top, the edge being reversed and the gathering made so as to form a pretty frilled heading; it is sewed to the yoke flatly on the outside. The lower edge is also gathered and stayed by a narrow strip of the goods. It is joined to the top of the skirt, which is gathered all round. A hem finishes the bottom of the skirt and a belt is adjusted over the seam joining the skirt and body, its ends being closed with buttonholes and buttons at one side of the front.

Lace or embroidered flouncing may be used for the skirt and net or webbing to match for the remainder of the dress, or for

the yoke and sleeves alone. A sash of ribbon may be worn instead of the belt, though the belt will be preferred when the dress is to be worn by a boy. Ginghams, seersuckers, cambrics, lawns, sateens, foulards, prints, percales and all kinds of wash goods will be made up into such dresses for Summer wear; the yoke may be of fancy tucking, lace net or embroidered webbing or of the material, as preferred. Woolens of all suitable varieties will be similarly made up, and so will China and pongee silks, Surah, etc.

Children from one to six years of age will look most attractive in the dress made from Pattern No. 1431.

1887 Little Girls' Costume

No. 1432. — Novel and picturesque is this little costume, which is here pictured made of cashmere and Surah. A charming vest composed of a little, pointed yoke and a full portion that droops in Molière fashion shows the two materials and is adjusted upon a wide under-front portion that extends across to fasten to a narrow under-front portion at the opposite side with buttonholes and buttons. The jacket fronts flare widely to expose the vest, and below the vest are cut across for a short distance and shaped to form two long, narrow tabs. Side-back gores and a curving center seam adjust the back gracefully to the form and all the seams are terminated below the waistline, the side-backs falling in tabs of depth corresponding with those of the jacket fronts. The backs, which are very long, are caught up to form loops and then tied in a knot over the center seam, the ends spreading in bow fashion. The tabs are trimmed with short rows of soutache braid of varying lengths extending upward from the lower edges, the tops of the rows being ornamented with tiny buttons. Rows of similar braid overtie the yoke nearly to its lower edge, the lower ends of the rows being likewise tipped with tiny buttons. The front edges of the jacket fronts show a pretty arrangement of braid extending in short rows backward from the front edges to the tops of the tabs, the rows being graduated in length so as to form a series of points and their back ends being tipped with buttons. A little standing collar finishes the neck in the approved fashion. A charming feature of the costume is the novel effect produced by the long and short sleeves. The short sleeves are prettily curved at their lower edges and produce the effect of deep caps; the long sleeves are full and have narrow bands at their wrists. The long sleeves are of Surah with a frill of lace at the edges of the bands; the short sleeves are of the cashmere and are trimmed with braid and buttons to correspond with the rest of the costume. A frill of lace is worn at the neck.

The skirt is gathered at the top and joined to the under-fronts and vest, and back of these to a yoke that fits smoothly under the back and is tacked to the center and side-back seams. A hem finishes the bottom of the skirt and decoration is not added.

Pattern No. 1432 is for girls from three to seven years old.

The wide-brimmed hat is trimmed with ribbon which falls in short streamers at the back.

LITTLE GIRLS' COSTUME.

1432
Front View.

1432
Back View.

1887 Girls' Dress and Cap

This consists of a Little Girls' dress No. 1522 and Cap No. 1519.

The dress is here shown developed in embroidered nun's-vailing. The waist has only side and shoulder shaping seams and is gathered at the bottom nearly to the seams and finished with a belt. It is closed at the back with buttonholes and small buttons and the neck is finished with a standing collar. To the bottom of the waist is joined the full skirt, which is gathered all round at the top and has only a hem finish at its edge. The sleeves have a slight fullness across their tops, and at the bottom are gathered to cuff-like wristbands that are shaped at the top to form a point at the back of the wrists and are wide enough to slip easily over the hand. Ruffs of lace are added at the neck and wrists.

Cambric, lawn, sateen, chambray, gingham, prints, seersucker, China, India, Surah and Summer silks of all varieties, cashmere, serge, flannel, etc., are all suitable for dresses of this style. Flouncing may be used for the skirt, with plain or embroidered goods of light texture for the body.

The little cap is made of pale blue China silk. Its crown is smooth and tapers narrowly toward the bottom, while the front is full and is made to stand high in a picturesque manner by box-plaits in its front edge and side-plaits in its back edge. An interlining of crinoline is usually added to preserve the shape and a lining of the silk finishes the cap. The crown lining is similar in shape to the crown, but the lining of the front portion is plain along the front edge and has only enough plaits in its back edge to produce an easy fit. The cap is piped at the edges with the silk, and a piping is also inserted in the seam joining the crown and front. A frill of lace affords a soft, dainty finish about the face and ribbon ties are bowed under the chin. A ribbon bow is also fastened to the bottom of the crown.

LITTLE GIRLS' DRESS AND CAP.

1522
Front View.

1522
Back View.

LITTLE GIRLS' DRESS WITH SPENCER WAIST.

1888
Ladies' Fashions

House Dress, Parasol and Bodice.

1888 Ladies' Costumes

Walking Dress, Hat and Sleeve.

1888
Ladies' Dress

This is a promenade costume made in figured and plain China-silk, challis, sateen or dotted black lace. The entire skirt is covered with three kilt-plaited flounces of the figured material. If of black lace, each flounce has three rows of narrow black watered ribbon. If of China-silk or challis, ribbon to match the prevailing color. If made of sateen, the flounces will be untrimmed. The back-drapery is short and full; it may be either figured or plain like the bodice. The long-pointed bodice laces at the back but this is purely optional, as the style can be preserved by buttoning down the front. The vandyked tabs from the shoulders and the epaulettes are of the figured material. Hat to correspond.

1888
Ladies' Dress

Here is a pretty and simple model for a gingham. The skirt is plait or else in large kilt-plaits. The overdrapery is all in one piece, two widths of gingham being joined and then used crosswise. The looping may be done from the illustration. The bodice has a vest of plain gingham or sateen to match the prevailing color of the plaid. It forms a short postillion at the back. Cuffs and collar of the plain.

1888
Ladies' Costume

This is a stylish model for a gown of tennis-flannel. These flannels are mostly in stripes of delicate colors, wash well and are very light in texture. The skirt of this gown is laid in large kilt-plaits. The overdrapery is long and all in one piece. The bodice is pointed front, with a short postillion-back. It has long coat-sleeves quite large at the top and a high standing collar. The underskirt of this gown is kilted upon a yoke without foundation-lining, the kilts kept in place by being taped.

1888 Ladies' Breakfast Gown

Illustrated is a pretty breakfast-gown, of which we only give the upper part. The double box-plait of the back is confined at the waist. The loose fronts are kept in place by the belt and sash of ribbon. Lace trims the neck and front, also the sleeves. This model may be used simply for a breakfast-sacque, and can be made of cashmere or China-silk in any self-color, with white or black lace and colored ribbon to match. These sacques are very useful over an old black silk skirt. Black cashmere trimmed with black lace and cardinal-red ribbon is both pretty, stylish, and becoming — and, above all, most useful.

1888
Girls' Costume

For a girl of four years we give a cream flannel frock, plaited back and front in fine kilts. The collar and sleeves match. The sash is of plaid ribbon and is tied at the back. The hat is of cream-white straw, trimmed with loops of narrow ribbon.

1888
Girls' Dress

For a girl of ten to twelve years we have a kilted skirt of plaid gingham or woolen, with an overdress of pin-striped to match in color. The top part of the full sleeves is of the stripe, while the deep cuffs are of the plaid. The hat is of straw, faced with velvet and trimmed with ostrich-tips and loops of ribbon.

1888
Child's Outfit

This Blouse-apron is for a child of two to three years. It is made of plain chambrey gingham, trimmed with four rows of narrow white cotton braid.

1889 Ladies' Round Waist

Figure No. 323 G. — Ladies' Round Waist.

Challis and velvet are combined in the present instance, with trimmings of *crêpe lisse*, ribbon and velvet. The shaping of the waist is effected by double bust darts, underarm and side-back gores and a center seam. Upon the front linings are arranged fronts that are shirred at the shoulders, where they are included in the seams; they are also shirred at the waistline at each side of the closing, which is made invisibly down the center. The sleeves are in coat-sleeve style; each is completed at the wrist with an upturned frill of *crêpe lisse*, while at the top is a full puff that rises high above the shoulders. The neck, which is cut slightly low in front, is finished with a rolling collar of velvet, below which a bow of ribbon and a jabot of *lisse* fall over the closing and decorate the front of the waist. The lower part of the waist is passed beneath the top of

the skirt, and about the waist is worn a plaited belt of velvet that is held in place by three fancy pins at the left side.

As part of a costume or otherwise the mode will develop nicely in almost all grades of fabrics; it is particularly favorable to foulards, Henriettas, etc. All the light-weight Summer goods will also make up prettily in this way. Trimming may be applied as preferred.

The lace toque is prettily trimmed with flowers.

1889
Ladies Bodice

Figure No. 322 G. — Ladies' Low-Necked Waist.

Cameo-pink Surah is the material here pictured and smocking provides the decoration. The full outside portion is arranged upon smooth portions that are adjusted by double bust darts, underarm and side-back gores and a center seam; it is smocked a little below the upper edge to pointed yoke depth,

the tackings being made far enough from the edge to form a pretty frill. The fullness is confined at the waistline by two rows of gathers, a belt being applied between the rows; the waist is held in place by a ruffle sewed to its lower edge and passed under the top of the skirt. The short, puffed sleeves are each gathered at the upper edge and smocked a little above the lower edge to form a frill. A sash of Surah encircles the waist.

The ornamental effect of smocking, now so popular, is nicely illustrated by the mode, although shirring or tucking may be substituted, with good effect. China and India silks, Surah, etc., are the most popular materials for bodices of this description, which will show to good advantage over a guimpe of lace or silk mull.

1889
Ladies' Blouse

Figure No. 324 G. — Ladies' Blouse.

In this instance cream Surah, moiré and lace net were selected for the waist and lace net provides the garniture. The adjustment is performed by double bust darts, underarm and side-back gores and a center seam. Over the fronts are arranged low blouse-fronts that are shirred a little below the upper edge, the fullness forming a frill at the top. Upon the backs and the underarm and side-back gores is arranged a blouse back that is correspondingly shirred and joined to the blouse fronts in short seams over the shoulders, this arrangement revealing in yoke shape the upper part of the waist which is faced with net. Over the coat sleeves are full puffs which are gathered at the upper and lower edges; the wrist of each sleeve is completed with a pointed cuff of moiré. In the present instance the standing collar is omitted, the neck finish consisting of a downward-turning frill of *lisse*. The lower part of the blouse is slipped beneath the top of the skirt; about the waist is worn a belt, the ends of which are secured with two fancy pins.

The mode is especially appropriate for the development of rich materials. The popular union of silks and lace shows to great advantage in this style of garment, although the pattern will develop equally well in numerous other combinations. A pretty waist may be made of pale-green faille with sleeves and facings of Valenciennes lace; in this case the cuffs and belt may be of velvet and a standing collar of the same may be substituted for the frill here pictured. When one material is used throughout, the cuffs, belt and collar may be decorated with fancy stitching or rows of narrow moiré ribbon.

The hat is a flat shape, turned up at the back and trimmed with a wreath of flowers.

Figure No. 323 G.

Figure No. 322 G.   LADIES' BODICES.   Figure No. 324 G.

Figure No. 322 G illustrates Pattern No. 2786 Figure No. 323 G illustrates Pattern No. 2799
Figure No. 324 G illustrates Pattern No. 2795

No. 2803   No. 2787

1889
Ladies' Costume

No. 2803. — This costume is pictured made of figured sateen and velvet, with lace edging and a ribbon bow for garniture.

Figured foulard and velvet are here united, with facings of velvet and embroidery in two widths for decorations. The four-gored skirt of lining is entirely concealed by its ample draperies, the graceful outlines of which are preserved by the use of reeds, although the wearing of a long, slender bustle will be found equally effective. The front-drapery extends over the front and right side gores and is wrinkled by a group of seven forward-turning plaits at the left side and six similar plaits at the right side of the center at the top, and by two clusters of three upturning plaits each in the right side edge. Over the left side-gore the side-drapery presents jabot-folds that are the result of three backward-turning plaits. In the top of the back-drapery near each front edge is a bournous; between these loops the upper edge is gathered, and at the center near the belt two upturning plaits form slight cascades. A forward-turning row of wide embroidery trims the left side-gore, this trimming concealing the only exposed portion of the skirt and falling over the left side of the front-drapery.

The basque is fitted at the sides and back by under-arm and side-back gores and a curving center seam which terminates in a point. The fronts are fitted by double bust darts, and over the right front is adjusted a full ornamental-front, the darts in which are taken up with those in the front. The ornamental front is gathered half-way down the shoulder edge and at the lower edge to a little back of the front edge; the right front overlaps the left front, the closing being made with buttons and buttonholes in a fly. A velvet revers is joined to the front edge of the left front; between the fronts is inserted a chemisette that is attached permanently at one side. A high standing collar is at the neck. A frill of narrow embroidery is sewed along the front edge of the outside front and continued in a row about the neck at the back and in a frill along the front edge of the left front. The sides arch high over the hips and the basque is pointed at the center of the front. The sleeve foundations are in coat-sleeve shape and the upper portions are larger than their linings; the puff effect characteristic of the Hading style is produced by gathers at the upper edge and at the side edges from a little below the top. A velvet cuff-facing trimmed at the top by an upturned row of narrow edging forms the wrist decoration.

2803
Right Side-Front View.

If a V opening at the neck be desired, the collar and chemisette may be omitted. Challis, tamise, nun's-vailing, sateen, batiste, Surah, silk muslin, mull, India silk, Benga-line, brilliantine, etc., may be developed by the mode, with lace, velvet, passementerie, ribbon, Persian bands, etc., for trimming.

2803
Left Side-Back View.

1889
Ladies' Costume

2787
Side-Front View.

2787
Side-Back View.

No. 2787. — This costume may be seen developed in plain dress goods, striped Surah and velvet with trimmings of velvet ribbon and lace.

The costume is here shown made of figured tulle and moiré and moiré ribbon provides the garniture. The foundation skirt, which is of lining silk, is in the standard walking shape, and desirable outlines may be secured for the drapery either by the use of a long, slender bustle or by the adjustment of reeds. The front-drapery covers the gores and extends a short distance on the back-breadth, where it is sewed to position; its fullness is disposed of by a row of shirring at its upper edge and a corresponding row a short distance below. The plaited back-drapery is arranged in four backward-turning plaits in the upper edge at each side of the center; its side edges are sewed along the corresponding edges of the front-drapery. Both draperies are trimmed near their lower edges with five rows of narrow moiré ribbon.

Over the plaited back-drapery is another back-drapery, one side edge of which is sewed along the side-back seams while the opposite edge is sewed along the side edges of the other draperies, the arrangement producing the effect of a scarf. This drapery is then gathered closely at the center and attached to the center seam of the basque with a hook and loop.

The basque fronts are shaped by double bust darts; upon them are arranged front ornaments that are gathered at the shoulders, where they are included in the seams. The ornaments were also gathered at the neck edge, and again at the lower edge, where they are sewed to the fronts a little above the waistline. To these ornaments are applied revers that are included in the shoulder seams, from which they taper to points, serving as a pretty framing for the ornaments, which they reveal between them with plastron effect. The remainder of the adjustment is performed by underarm, side and side-back

seams and a center seam; the lower outline describes a point at the back. At the neck is a standing collar which is extended to close at the left side. The full upper portions of the fanciful sleeves are gathered at the upper and lower edges; the wrists are finished with narrow cuffs that flare at the inside of the arm. A full puff of tulle encircled at the center with a narrow ribbon is sewed underneath to the lower part of the sleeve. A deep, shaped girdle encircles the basque at the waistline, being reversed at its upper edge and closed beneath the roll at the center of the back with a hook and loop.

The mode will be much admired for the development of light, airy fabrics, also for cashmere, Henrietta, challis or any of the soft, clinging materials. Narrow moiré or velvet ribbon is the favored decoration and, when of a pretty contrasting shade, it adds greatly to the dressy effect of the costume.

1889 Ladies' Watteau Wrapper

This illustrates a Ladies' wrapper. — No. 2806.

Foulard showing large figures in olive upon a pink background was here chosen for the wrapper, with olive velvet ribbon and lace edging in two widths for garnitures. The fronts close their depth with buttons and buttonholes; in each side are single bust darts which, with underarm and side-back gores and a center seam, effect a graceful adjustment. The Watteau is formed of a separate section that is laid in a double box-plait, the top of which is placed even with the neck; the back of the Watteau is deepened to form an oval train. A high standing collar provides the finish at the neck; over it falls a frill of narrow lace edging. The coat sleeves are each completed at the wrist by a narrow cuff-facing of velvet ribbon that flares slightly and shows a frill of narrow edging. The wrapper is trimmed at the front and sides with a deep frill of lace edging surmounted by velvet ribbon. Long ties of velvet ribbon are included in the side seams at the waistline and arranged in long loops and ends at the front.

When the garment is intended for dressy wear, India and China silks, foulards, etc., are usually selected for it. It will however, make up well in challis, cashmere, serge and numerous other wool fabrics, for which narrow moiré ribbon will provide an effective garniture.

LADIES' WATTEAU WRAPPER.

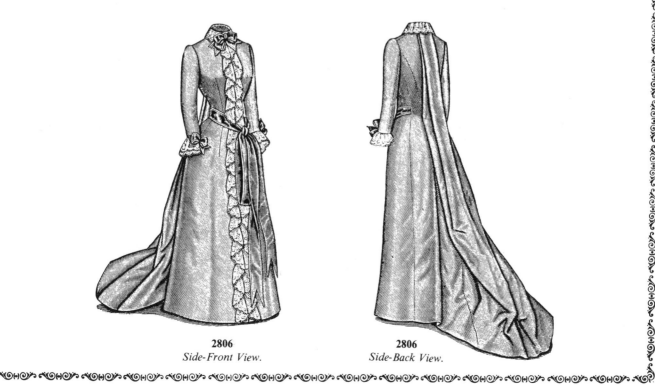

2806
Side-Front View.

2806
Side-Back View.

1889
Misses' Dress

No. 2788. — At figure No. 332 G this dress is shown developed in dull-rose tamise and olive-green velvet, with trimmings of Genoese-point lace and two widths of olive velvet ribbon.

In the present instance the dress is pictured made of figured challis and velvet, and trimmed with cordings of velvet and white lace. The low-necked body is fitted by single bust darts and underarm gores, and the closing is made with buttons and buttonholes through the center of a broad box-plait laid in the back edge of the right back. A box-plait is correspondingly laid at the center of the front, where the lower outline is somewhat deepened; the neck is rounded low at the front and back and finished with shapely collar-portions that curve to points above the box-plait in front and are deepest where they meet with square ends and a rounding lower outline above the closing at the back. The puffed sleeves, which are made over plain linings, have two plaits laid in each end where they are seamed under the arms and are finished at the lower edge with a cording of velvet. The full skirt hangs in graceful folds, its upper edge being gathered all round and joined to the body, and its lower edge completed by a deep hem. A cording of velvet is inserted in the seaming of the skirt to the body, and the lower edge of each collar portion is trimmed by a deep frill of lace edging that is continued in a pretty jabot at each side of the box-plait in front.

Combinations of velvet or silk with challies, sateens, vailings and similar fabrics will be favored for these dresses, but one material will also make up satisfactorily. When washable goods are used, all-over embroidery or wide insertion will be selected for the collar portions, embroidered flouncing for the skirt and plain lawn for the other portions.

Figure No. 332 G. MISSES' DRESS.

2788
Front View.

2788
Back View.

MISSES' DRESS. (To be Worn with a Guimpe.)

1889 Girls' Sailor Costume

Figure No. 328 G. — This illustrates a Girls' costume.

Dove-colored serge and electric-blue velvet are combined in the present instance, with velvet ribbon in two widths and velvet for trimming. The kilt skirt is joined to a smooth, sleeveless lining, which is fitted by under-arm and shoulder seams, the front being faced in V shape and trimmed with rows of narrow velvet ribbon that are pointed at the center.

The loosely fitting blouse is adjusted by shoulder and under-arm seams, the fullness at the waist being confined by an elastic cord inserted in a narrow hem at the lower edge. The neck is cut in V shape and is finished with a sailor collar that falls squarely at the back and tapers to points in front, where a bow of wide velvet ribbon is ornamentally placed. The coat sleeves are trimmed at the wrists with velvet cuff-facings.

Flannel, outing-cloth, serge, cashmere, gingham, lawn, etc., will make up effectively in this way, with velvet ribbon, Persian bands, braid, etc., for trimming. A very stylish costume may be made of dull-rose all-wool Surah and myrtle-green velvet, gilt cord supplying the decoration.

The straw hat is a wide-brimmed sailor shape and is trimmed with a band of ribbon matching the velvet in the costume.

Figure No. 328 G. — GIRLS' SAILOR COSTUME.

2810
Front View.

2810
Back View.

1889
Girls' Dress

No. 2784. — At Figure No. 327 G may be observed developed in tamise and trimmed with braid, fancy buttons and narrow and wide Irish-point embroidery.

In the present instance the dress is pictured made of blue gingham, white cambric and insertion, with narrow Hamburg edging and small buttons for decorations. The round waist is shaped by shoulder and under-arm seams and closes at the back with buttons and buttonholes.

The front is laid in seven narrow, forward-turning tucks at each side of the center, and at the back at each side of the closing are made three backward-turning tucks of similar width. Upon the front, and included in the shoulder and underarm seams, are jacket fronts; they are each cut away above the bust to describe a point at each side, and the front edge of the shallow portion is decorated with five small pearl buttons. The lower edges of the jacket fronts are trimmed with narrow Hamburg edging, which is continued up the front edge to the notch. The sleeves, which have but one seam, are in two portions; the upper portion is gathered at the top and extended to the elbow, where it meets the tucked lower-portion, a cording being inserted in the joining. Wristbands showing a tiny frill of edging at their lower edges provide the completion at the wrists. A standing collar similarly trimmed is at the neck. Sash-ties that are each laid in three upward-turning plaits and inserted in the under-arm seams are bowed at the back. The full skirt is hemmed at its lower edge and is joined to the lower edge of the body, the jacket fronts being left loose.

The simplicity of the mode makes it especially suitable for washable fabrics; it will also make up effectively in woolen or silken textures either singly or in combination. For dressy wear Surah or China silk will usually be selected, lace and ribbon being chosen for trimmings. Fancy stitching will form a dainty garniture for cashmere, serge and flannel school dresses, when only one material is used.

1889 Girls' Dress

No. 327 G. — This illustrates a girls' dress, No. 2784.

The dress is here pictured made of tamise, the trimmings consisting of fancy buttons, braid and two widths of Irish-point embroidery. The full, round skirt is trimmed at its lower edge with a row of wide embroidery; its upper edge is gathered and sewed to the body which is adjusted by underarm and shoulder seams and closed at the back with

Figure No. 327 G.

2784
Front View.

2784
Back View.

Figure No. 327 G. — GIRLS' DRESS.

buttons and buttonholes. Over the front, which is tucked, are arranged square jacket-fronts that are notched above the bust; above the notches the jacket fronts are trimmed with strips of braid, and below the bust they are decorated with three buttons. At the neck is a standing collar, trimmed with a row of narrow embroidery. The upper portion of each sleeve is gathered at the top and trimmed above the lower edge with three rows of braid; the lower portion is tucked, the lower edge being completed with a narrow wristband decorated with a falling frill of narrow embroidery. The plaited front ends of sash-ties are sewed to the underarm seams just above the joining of the skirt to the body, and the ties are arranged in a graceful bow at the back.

The fashion may be developed in all varieties of cotton and wool goods such as gingham, batiste, mull, cambric, sateen, cashmere, Henrietta, merino, etc.; and lace, embroidery, braid or ribbon may serve as decoration. A pretty dress may be made of red and white embroidered flouncing and Turkey-red lawn, narrow embroidered lawn edging decorating the collar and wristbands, and following the free edges of the jacket fronts.

Pattern No. 2784 is for girls from five to twelve years of age.

The wide-brimmed chip hat is trimmed with a full bow of fancy ribbon matching the color of the dress.

1889
Girls' Dress

No. 2644. — Cashmere, Surah and velvet are associated in this dress at Figure No. 466 D, velvet, embroidered bands and velvet ribbon forming the decoration.

In the present instance the dress is shown made of pink gingham and all-over embroidery, with trimmings of white Irish-point embroidery and fancy-edged satin ribbon. The fronts and back of the waist are arranged over plain lining-foundations, the front linings being adjusted to the form by single bust darts. The back of the waist is gathered along the upper and lower edge near the center, a similar gathering being made about belt-depth above the lower row; the adjustment is made by shoulder and under-arm seams. A plastron of Irish-point embroidery is displayed between the fronts, the right side edge being sewed permanently to the right front-lining. The fronts are turned under at their front edges and have two backward-turning plaits laid just back of the front edges, and the lower portion is gathered almost to the under-arm seam. The fronts are in surplice style. A deep frill of embroidery is arranged at the back below the high standing collar, which closes at the left shoulder. The embroidery is continued across the shoulders and down the fronts beneath the second plait, terminating midway between the bust and waist-line. Over the sleeves, which are in coat-sleeve style, are arranged ornamental sleeves that reach to the elbow, where they each meet a full puff that is gathered at the top and bottom. Below the puff the sleeve is overlaid with an upturned row of embroidered edging, which resembles a deep cuff. The front linings are closed down the center with hooks and loops, and the plastron is attached to the left front-lining with hooks and loops. The skirt is full and is shirred twice across the front. At the back it is laid in two double box-plaits, and a hem finishes the lower edge. A long panel is arranged on the skirt at each side of the center of the front, affording ample opportunity for contrasts by being prettily lined in some harmonizing shade. It is sewed to the lower edge of the body and belt, the latter being applied to the lower edge of the body on the outside. A ribbon is arranged about the waist and is tied at the back.

Plain or figured goods in either silken or woolen textures may be made up in this way, and one material may be used throughout, or contrasts may be effected by combining harmonious colors or textures. The dress may be effectively developed in cashmere, Surah, China silk, etc. In the arrangement of the plastron and surplice fronts there is abundant opportunity for pretty combinations. In a cloth or cashmere costume the vest may be braided in gold or silver, and the panels on the front of the skirt may be of velvet or faille and lined with any material in harmony with the rest of the garment.

We have pattern No. 2644 in seven sizes for girls from three to nine years of age.

2644

2644

Figure No. 466 D

1889
Misses' Basque
(In Directoire
Style)

No. 2792. — In this instance light and dark dress goods are combined. The basque has fronts that are closely fitted by single bust darts and closed with hooks and loops. The right front is extended; upon it is arranged a plastron that consists of a yoke upper part and a full lower-portion. The full portion is gathered at the top where it meets the yoke, the lower edge of which overlaps it. The fullness at the lower edge of the plastron is collected in a row of gathers and sewed firmly to the edge of the front, which extends only to the waistline where it is finished with a narrow binding that hides the sewing. The jacket fronts, which are double, are included in the shoulder and underarm seams and turned back in triangular revers that terminate slightly below the bust. Underarm and side-back gores and a curved center seam adjust the remainder of the basque; the center and side-back seams cease at the waistline to form tabs. The full upper-portions of the sleeves, which are gathered at their upper and lower edges, are arranged

2792
Front View.

2792
Back View.

upon coat-shaped linings, and the lower edge of each sleeve is completed by a cuff that flares at the outside seam. A high standing collar provides the fashionable finish at the neck. A girdle that is laid in four upward-turning plaits is joined to the right front at the underarm seam; it is adjusted upon a plain lining, and the closing is invisibly effected at the left side with hooks and loops.

The basque may be developed in almost any variety of material and may form part of a costume or contrast with the skirt, as preferred. The mode affords opportunity for effective color blendings and contrasts in materials; three different fabrics may be associated when a fanciful effect is desired. A pretty development of the mode is in green cloth with the collar, plastron and cuffs of tan cloth. Three large fancy steel buttons are placed on each jacket front just below the reversed portion.

1889
Girls' Apron

No. 2783. — The apron is here repre-sented made of white lawn and embroidered edging; tucks and embroidered edging in two widths provide the trimming. The side-backs and side-fronts are joined by underarm and short shoulder seams and overlap the center-backs and center-front respectively, the body being given a Pompadour outline by the arrangement of the parts. Each arm's-eye is outlined by a frill of narrow embroi-dered edging; the closing is made with hooks and loops. The upper edge of the skirt is gathered and joined to the lower edge of the body, from which it hangs in free folds, its back edges being hemmed. The lower part is trimmed with a row of deep, embroidered edging below a cluster of four tucks, the material being cut away from beneath the embroidery.

The tucks should be made before cutting the skirt out. Insertion may be substituted for the tucks, if preferred. Any material used for children's aprons and a number of dress fabrics will develop well by this pattern, and any simple finish may be adopted.

Pattern No. 2783 is for girls from five to twelve years old.

GIRLS' APRON.

1889 Little Girls' Dress

No. 2782. — Gingham and white fancy tucking are here united in the dress, with buttons, cambric bands and white embroidered edging for trimmings. The skirt consists of joined straight widths; its lower edge is deeply hemmed. The upper edge, which is joined to the round body, is gathered, and the shaping of the body is performed by shoulder and underarm seams. The front and backs are cut out and extended to meet in short seams upon the shoulders. A Pompadour yoke, the lower outline of which is rounding at the back and square at the front, is inserted between the deeper portions of the front and backs. The backs are gathered twice along their lower edges at each side of the closing and once along their upper edges, and the joining of the front and backs to the Pompadour is concealed by a falling frill of embroidered edging surmounted by a tiny cambric band. Over the shallow part of the waist in the front is arranged a shaped ornamental section that is held in place at each side by three small buttons. Beneath the side edges of this section are sewed the plaited ends of sash-ties that are bowed in loops and ends at the back of the dress. The neck is neatly completed by a standing collar that is trimmed with an upward-turning frill of embroidered edging above a tiny band of cambric. The sleeves, which are in shirt-sleeve style, are finished with deep cuffs that are trimmed at the lower edge with a cambric band and a falling frill of embroidered edging.

A fancy for striking color blendings may be freely indulged by making the Pompadours of material in some contrasting shade. Batiste, lace-striped gingham, etc., are now the favored washable fabrics for children's dresses, and pretty harmonies in color are produced in the stripes. The mode may also be suitably developed in some of the soft wool goods in combination with Surah or faille; in such case the Pompadours, sash-ties, cuffs, etc., will be of silk. A pretty dress is of old-rose cashmere with the ties of wide moiré ribbon to match, and velvet for the cuffs, ornament and collar.

2782
Front View.

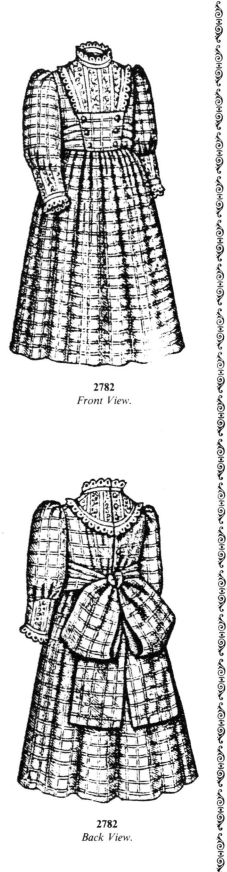

2782
Back View.

2783
Front View.

2783
Back View.

1889
Girls' Apron

No. 2785. — The apron is here shown made of nainsook; embroidered edging in two widths and all-over embroidery supply the decoration. The skirt is trimmed at its lower edge with a row of wide embroidered edging; its upper edge is gathered and sewed to the lower edge of the body, which is adjusted by underarm and short shoulder seams and closed at the back with buttons and buttonholes. The neck is cut low and decorated with an upward-turning row of narrow embroidered edging, which is carried down the front over the outer edges of a V-shaped facing of all-over embroidery to the waistline. The arms'-eyes are also decorated with narrow embroidered edging.

The apron may be prettily developed in lawn, linen, nainsook, cambric, dimity, cross-barred muslin or fancy open-work gingham; and Medici, torchon, Valenciennes and crochetted lace, embroidered edging, etc., may provide the decoration.

This apron was developed to be worn by girls from two to eight years of age.

LITTLE GIRLS' APRON.

2785
Back View.
LITTLE GIRLS' APRON.

2785
Front View.
LITTLE GIRLS' APRON.

1889
Girls' Costume

No. 9307. — The charming novelty of this costume does not detract from its practicality, as the mode is adapted to all varieties of seasonable dress goods. Cashmere is the material shown in the present instance and satin is daintily introduced as a garniture. The costume has a yoke-shaped upper portion that is adjusted by seams upon the shoulders, hemmed at its right front edge and underfaced at the left; to this the remainder of the costume is sewed with something of the "Mother, Hubbard" effect, some very attractive departures from the latter mode being, however, introduced. Three sections are united in the main portion of the garment by curving side seams. The widest section forms the back; at its center a double box-plait is folded, enough extra length being allowed to extend the plait to the top of the yoke. The upper edge is turned in for a finish at each side of the plait and is shirred three times, only about a quarter of an inch being allowed between the shirrings. A double box-plait is folded at the closing edge of the right front and extended to the top of the yoke in the same manner as at the center of the back, and the edge back of it is turned in and similarly shirred nearly to the arm's-eye. The left closing edge is hemmed and the top is shirred to accord with the right side, the plait in the latter, of course, coming directly at the center of the front where the closing, which is performed with hooks and eyes, is made. The upper and lower rows of shirrings are sewed through to the yoke, and the center-front plait is stitched in its folds for its entire depth, while that at the back is sewed only to a little below the waistline. Beneath the folds of the back plait, just above where its seam terminates, are sewed belt sections of satin, the free ends of which are fastened in front with a fancy buckle. The sleeves are in coat shape and have dainty cuff-facings of satin at the wrists. A standing collar of cashmere is at the neck; in the same seam with it is sewed a round, flat collar of satin.

The charming suggestion of a Watteau given by the plait at the back is enhanced when figured foulards, sateens and China silks are chosen for the costume. Any other material deemed more desirable may, however, be selected, with the assurance of a satisfactory result. Sometimes the yoke will be in contrast with the lower portion.

This costume can be worn by girls from one to nine years of age.

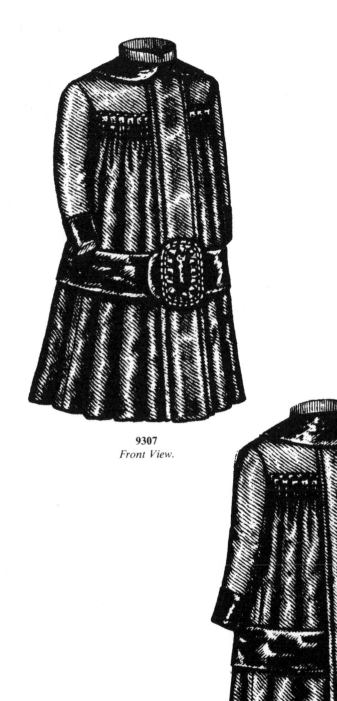

9307
Front View.

9307
Back View.

1889 Girls' Directoire Costume

No. 2813. — The costume is here shown made of golden brown foulé, white silk and brown velvet, the decorations consisting of velvet, fancy buttons, cord and applique. The round skirt is box-plaited at the front and sides, and the back is gathered and sewed to a short band that is tacked underneath to the seams of the over-dress at the waistline; the upper edge of the front and sides is joined to the short fronts which are closed with buttons and buttonholes. Upon the fronts is adjusted a vest that is gathered once at its upper and lower edges, the lower gathers being stylishly concealed by a strap that is overlaid with applique. A similar strap is placed over the vest at the bust, heightening its puffed effect.

The over-dress is adjusted in the usual way. The side-backs show a plait a little below the waistline. The back falls in long coat-tails, the center seam ending at the waistline. The jacket fronts are of basque depth and are reversed above the bust to form tiny revers which are faced with velvet. On the front edge of each jacket front, in a line with the end of each strap on the vest, are placed three buttons over the front ends of simulated cord buttonholes. At the neck is a high standing collar overlaid with applique and a flat collar falls stylishly over the backs. The leg-o'-mutton sleeves are trimmed at the wrists with cuff facings of velvet, which are also decorated with applique.

The costume may be prettily developed in all sorts of materials of either woolen or silken texture, combinations being especially suited to the mode. Henrietta cloth, tamise, cashmere, challis, India silk, Surah, etc., will make up nicely in this way. Persian bands, Genoese-point lace, velvet, passementerie, etc., may form the trimming.

The brim of the straw hat flares from the face; ribbon and ostrich tips provide the decoration.

Five to twelve-year-old girls will look most attractive in this costume.

1889
Girls' Dress

No. 2866. — This dress is illustrated made of robin's egg blue cashmere and dark blue velvet, with trimmings of velvet. The full, round skirt has a deep hem at the bottom, above which are two deep tucks; at the upper edge it is gathered and sewed to the body, which is fitted by underarm and side-back gores, the closing being effected in the back with buttons and buttonholes. The neck of the backs is cut in low, round outline. The fronts are reversed at the top to form a V and are faced with velvet, the revers falling prettily over the surplice fronts, which cross in the characteristic way. The short, puffed sleeves are finished with ornaments that are pointed on the upper side. A sash encircles the waist.

Dresses of this kind may be developed in any soft wool goods, foulé, Henrietta cloth, cashmere, tamise, challis and all-wool Surah being particularly adaptable; embroidery, ribbon, lace, etc. may supply the trimming. Narrow braid may be applied on each tuck. Washable fabrics will also make up attractively, although the contrasts are particularly pretty between the white guimpe (which may be made as fanciful as desired) and the soft shades that are now so popular in woolen fabrics.

This is an attractive pattern for girls from five to twelve years of age.

2866
Front View.

2866
Back View.

GIRLS' DRESS. (TO BE WORN WITH A GUIMPE.)

1889
Girls' Dress

No. 2837. — Figured challis was selected for this dress with a Surah sash and plaitings of mull providing the decoration. The dress is here pictured made of olive green cashmere and dark green velvet; Surah, velvet and fringe provide the trimming. The full, round skirt, which is gathered at its upper edge, is laid in kilt-plaits that turn toward the back, the arrangement producing a box-plait at the front. The skirt is joined to the body, which is fitted by single bust darts and underarm and side-back gores, the closing being performed invisibly at the back. The fronts are arranged in five forward-turning plaits at each side of the center; the fullness is confined at the waistline by two rows of shirring. The backs have five similar forward-turning plaits at each side of the closing. The fullness at the waistline is confined by shirring. The front and back are each adjusted over linings. At the neck is a high standing collar. On each of the coat sleeves is arranged a puff that is laid in six backward-turning plaits above the elbow. The exposed part of the sleeve is faced with velvet. A Surah sash, the ends of which are trimmed with deep knotted fringe, is carried around

2837
Front View.

2837
Back View.

the waist and tied in a graceful bow at the back.

The dress may be developed in all kinds of woolen and washable goods, all-wool Surah, French challis, nun's-vailing, foulé, tamise and camelette being favored. The

trimming may be provided by velvet, silk, embroidery, lace, fringe, etc. Silk will develop handsomely in this way and velvet may be used for the collar and cuffs.

This attractive dress is appropriate for girls from three to nine years old.

1889
Girls' Apron

No. 2895. — In the present instance embroidered flouncing and nainsook are united with narrow embroidery for garniture. The full skirt is gathered and sewed to the body and is made of flouncing. The fronts and backs are joined by seams at the sides and are gathered once at the upper edges and twice at the lower edges for a short distance at each side of the center of the front and of the closing. The upper gatherings are tacked to stays that extend over the shoulders and are joined by short seams. Extended portions are covered with full puffs. Narrow embroidered edgings trim the arm's-eye and neck edges of the apron, the edging on the front and back being continued across the ends of the puffs. A belt is sewed to the body between the gatherings at the waistline; the plaited ends of sash ties are sewed to the belt at each side, the ties being bows at the back.

Colored or white embroidered flouncing, percale, nainsook, lawn, barred muslin, cambric, linen, gingham, etc., will develop effectively in this way, with crocheted edging, ruffling embroidered edging or torchon, Medici or any washable lace for garniture. For general use blue or red embroidered flouncing or Turkey-red or blue cotton goods to correspond will unite very stylishly in the apron and wear most satisfactorily.

This is a pattern for two to eight-year-old girls.

1889
Girls' Dress

No. 2918. — The dress is here pictured developed in fancy dotted suit goods and light silk with velvet of a contrasting color for decoration. The full, round skirt is gathered and sewed to the body, which is shaped by underarm and shoulder seams. Over the lining are arranged an outside front and backs that are cut in V shape back and front, disclosing the full yoke, which is shirred at the upper part. A band of velvet outlines the edges of the V's and the standing collar is omitted. Over each of the shirt sleeves is an ornament that reaches to the elbow and is trimmed at its lower part with a band of velvet. The lower edge of the sleeve is finished with a wristband.

The mode is particularly adaptable to combinations, figured, plain or fancy silk and velvet uniting prettily with all soft wool fabrics.

Little girls from two to seven years of age can wear this costume.

2918
Front View.

2918
Back View.

1890
Ladies' Costume

No. 3332. — Dress goods, silk and velvet are stylishly combined in this instance, and silk cord and buttons form the decoration. The skirt, which is fashioned in the approved four-gored shape, is nearly concealed by draperies and will hang gracefully over a long, slender bustle. A drapery, that falls over the front and left side gores and laps slightly upon the right side-gore at the top, is disposed in graceful, sagging folds at the front by a group of forward-turning plaits in the top at each side of the center; a straight panel is arranged upon the right side-gore to lap upon the drapery at the top and flare from it to the bottom of the skirt, revealing the gore in V shape. The panel is turned back at its front edge to form a revers, which is faced with velvet, and back of the revers it is decorated near the top and bottom and midway between with groups of buttons arranged over the back ends of buttonholes simulated with silk cord.

The body of the over-dress is a basque smoothly adjusted by double bust darts, underarm and side-back gores and a well curved center seam; it is pointed at the center of the front and back, and upon the fronts, which are closed down with buttons and buttonholes, is arranged a stylish *gilet* prettily framed by tapering revers of velvet that are jointed to the side edges. The fullness of the *gilet* is draped in graceful, drooping folds by three forward-turning plaits folded in each shoulder edge. At the neck is a standing collar that matches the revers and is closed at the left shoulder seam, its upper and lower edges, and also the free edges of the revers, being outlined with pipings of silk cord. The stylish sleeves, which match the *gilet*, are made over coat-shaped linings. The fullness at the top of each upper sleeve portion is closely drawn by gathers in the upper edge to rise high above the shoulder, while below the elbow the sleeve fits smoothly over the arm to within a short distance of the wrist, where the inner seam is discontinued; below the seam the sleeve is under-faced with velvet and outlined at the free edges with silk cord, and it is further ornamented near the inner seam with buttons and simulated button-holes. A tasteful drapery that is closely gathered at its upper edge is sewed to the back of the basque on the outside and falls in natural folds over the back-breadth to the lower edge, its side edges being hemmed and tacked at intervals to the adjoining edges of the front-drapery and panel.

Henrietta cloth, camel's-hair, cashmere, foulé, lady's-cloth, challis, sateen, Summer silk, etc., may be made up effectively in this way, with India silk, Surah, *crêpe de chine*, etc., for the plastron. When the revers and facings are of the dress material they may be decorated with braiding, embroidery or passementerie to produce effective contrasts with other parts of the costume.

3332
Right Side-Front View.

LADIES' COSTUME.

3332
Left Side-Back View.

1890
Ladies' Costume

No. 3156. — Figured foulard and dark velvet are here combined in the costume, with velvet, velvet ribbon and white Vandyke lace for decorations. The foundation is in the popular four-gored shape, and its graceful hanging is secured by the wearing of a long, slender bustle. Falling over the gores is a full, straight drapery that is drawn by gathers in the upper edge and ornamented above the hem finishing the lower edge with five rows of velvet ribbon. Arranged at each side over the upper part of this drapery is a short panier that is draped by five backward-turning plaits at the belt and three upward-turning plaits in the side edge, which passes into the side-back seam. At the center of the front at the top, the paniers overlap slightly. The back-drapery is arranged by tackings to fall in handsome jabot-folds at each side; it is underfaced with the material for some distance from the side edge and decorated with three rows of velvet ribbon, and the remainder of the drapery is drawn by gathers at the top to hang in natural folds at the center.

The fronts of the basque are fitted by double bust darts and closed at the center with hooks and eyes, and upon each front is arranged a surplice ornament that is laid in three forward-turning plaits; these plaits are overlapped to form a point at the lower edge, and they flare to a little above the waistline, where they are tacked to the front, the fullness spreading above them in soft folds to the shoulder edge, which is closely drawn by gathers. An ornament of velvet applied to each front back of the surplice ornament tapers narrowly from the arm's-eye to the lower edge, and the portion of the fronts disclosed in V outline between the surplice ornaments is faced with velvet and decorated at each side with a row of Vandyke trimming. The backs are arranged upon lining portions that are fitted by side-back gores and a curving center seam; they correspond in effect with the surplice ornaments, their fullness being gathered at the shoulder edges and laid in two backward-turning plaits in front of each back edge from a little above the waistline to the lower edge. The plaits are tacked at intervals to the backs of lining, which are disclosed between the backs in V shape and are faced with velvet and ornamented at each side with a row of Vandyke trimming like the fronts. The adjustment of the basque is completed by underarm gores. The coat-shaped sleeves are each ornamented at the top by a fanciful puff that is closely drawn by gathers in the upper edge and is deeply pointed to the elbow; the fullness rises high above the shoulder and is laid in two small, upward-

3156
Side-Front View.
LADIES' COSTUME.

3156
Side-Back View.
LADIES' COSTUME.

turning plaits at the center and tacked to the sleeve lower down. Three downward-turning plaits are laid in each side edge of the puff; its pointed outline is followed by a band of velvet at each side; the wrist is trimmed with three rows of velvet ribbon. A standing collar at the neck is overlaid with an upturned row of Vandyke lace.

Light Summer silks, challies, sateens and many soft woolens in combination with velvet, Surah, armure, etc., are especially favored for the costume, and it will also make up stylishly in plain and plaided or striped goods of the same texture, with garnitures of passementerie or ribbons. The ornaments back of the surplice ornaments may be omitted in favor of any suitable decorations and the paniers will often be trimmed to accord with the draperies.

1890
Ladies' Dress

No. 3321. — Broken-plaid dress goods and velvet are associated in the present instance, and velvet ribbon provides the trimming. The foundation skirt is fashioned in the approved four-gored shape and will hang gracefully over a long, slender bustle; it is covered by an ample drapery ingeniously arranged to produce the effect of a front and back drapery; at the back the fullness is closely drawn by gathers at the top to hang with the effect of a waterfall-drapery over the breadth, while a deep backward-turning plait flaring diagonally in front of the gathers at each side presents the appearance of a separate drapery arranged over the gores and stylishly wrinkled at the front by three forward-turning plaits in front of the deep plait at each side. The lower part of the drapery is effectively trimmed with five rows of velvet ribbon of graduated widths.

The front and back of the waist are cut bias and terminate at the waistline. The front is arranged upon fronts of lining that are fitted by double bust darts and closed at the center with buttons and buttonholes, and its fullness is disposed in slight, graceful folds above the bust by three upward-turning plaits folded in each shoulder edge and flaring toward the center; it is shaped to fit smoothly over the lining below the bust and is closed invisibly at the left shoulder and underarm seams. The back is arranged upon backs of lining that are fitted by side-back gores and a center seam; the adjustment of the waist is completed by underarm gores. The velvet sleeves, which are stylishly full above the elbows and are narrowed to fit the arms nicely below, are made over coat-shaped linings; the fullness of each upper sleeve-portion is arranged by means of gathers in the upper edge and tackings made to the lining below to stand high across the shoulder and extend in soft folds at the back of the arm above the elbow. The standing collar at the neck is closed at the left shoulder seam. The lower part of the waist is worn beneath the top of the skirt and a wide ribbon, drawn to a point at the center of the front and tied to fall in long loops and ends at the center of the back, is arranged about the waist.

Most effective developments of this dress will be made in combinations of plaided or striped silks or woolens with plain fabrics of similar texture or with dark velvets. The drapery will sometimes be cut bias, as well as the waist, and in this event little or no decoration will be required, as the bias effect is in itself very ornamental.

3321
Side-Front View.
LADIES' DRESS.

3321
Side-Back View.
LADIES' DRESS.

1890
Ladies' Costume

No. 3280. — Combination and Decoration for Special Parts of a Ladies' Costume. — White silk embroidered *crêpe lisse* flouncing and white India silk form the choice combination calculated to bring out the dainty effect of this mode.

At Figure No. 9 the skirt is pictured, the full drapery falling with the effect of a flounce-drapery over the China silk foundation, which shows to advantage the rich embroidery of the drapery fabric.

The basque is illustrated at Figure No. 10. The full fronts are cut from the flouncing from which part of the edge has been omitted and flare over the fitted fronts of China silk. The lower edge is outlined by a wrinkled girdle of heliotrope silk that is closed under a buckle at the center of the front; and the silk collar is in standing style. The silk coat sleeves have each adjusted at the top a full puff of *lisse* like that on the fronts, and a ribbon harmonizing with the girdle encircles the arm at the lower edge of the puff and is arranged in a bow on the upper side. The introduction of this pretty color is tasteful and effective. A costume made in this way will be suitable for both street and dressy wear, as illustrated by the different combinations shown at the two figures.

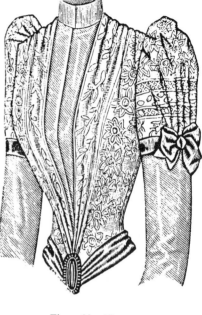

Figure No. 10.

Figure No. 9.

1890
Misses' Dress

No. 3113. — The dress is here pictured made of plaid gingham, embroidered edging and all-over embroidery; edging and ribbon supply the decoration. The full, low-necked front and backs, which are joined by a short seam on each shoulder, are arranged over a high-necked front and backs that are fitted by single bust darts and side-back gores and closed invisibly at the center of the back, the remainder of the adjustment being performed by underarm gores. The low-necked front and backs are turned under at the top, and the fullness is regulated by two rows of shirring at the top, where it forms a dainty frill. The fullness at the lower part is drawn toward the center of the front and the closing at the back by two rows of shirring and a belt is applied to the lower part of the body. The high-necked portions above the full portions are made of all-over embroidery, producing the effect of a guimpe, and at the neck is a standing collar of edging. The full sleeves, which are gathered at the upper and lower edges, have coat-shaped foundations, the exposed parts of which are made of all-over embroidery; the lower edge of each sleeve is trimmed with a frill of embroidered edging.

The popular four-gored skirt is used and a long, slender bustle is worn. Upon the skirt are arranged two deep flounces which cover it entirely; they are each hemmed deeply at the lower edge and gathered at the upper edge. The gathered edge of the lower flounce is sewed to the skirt a little above the knee and deeply overlapped by the upper one, and the top of the skirt is joined to the body. A ribbon encircles the waist and is tied at the left side of the front in long loops and ends.

A dress of this description will be especially liked for school wear; its simplicity and picturesque effect will render it generally popular. All sorts of cotton goods such as gingham, lawn, seersucker, zephyrs, cambric, mull, barred muslin and various other washable goods, will develop nicely by the mode; all-over embroidery may be united with any of these, or one material may be used throughout, as preferred, and lace, embroidery, etc., may supply the trimming.

This pattern has been designed for misses from ten to sixteen years of age.

1890
Misses' Dress

No. 3155. — Velvet and dress goods are here associated, with Surah for the sash and Vandyke lace for decoration. The skirt is in the four-gored style; the front-gore is trimmed at the bottom with deep, upturning Vandykes of velvet. Over the remainder of the skirt is arranged a full drapery that is laid in four forward-turning plaits over each side-gore, the front edges being turned under and tacked at intervals to the skirt, while at the back the top is drawn/in by gathers. Surplice fronts and backs, which are gathered at the shoulder and lower edges and crossed in the regulation fashion, are arranged over the fronts and back; the fronts are fitted by single bust darts and closed with buttons and buttonholes. Side-back gores and a curving center seam adjust the back and each side is made smooth by an underarm gore. The surplice portions at the back are included in the joining of the skirt and body; at the front the lower edge is finished with an underfacing and closed with a hook and eye. Arranged over the right surplice-front is an ornamental section, the back edge of which is inserted in the under-arm seam, while the front edge is cut in Vandykes, each point being tacked. Disclosed between the surplice fronts is a chemisette of velvet, which is sewed permanently to the left front at its side edge and inserted in the shoulder seam, the closing being made at the right side; the exposed part of the back is faced with velvet, the entire arrangement producing the effect of a V-shaped front and back. At the neck is a high standing collar which closes in a line with the chemisette at the shoulder edge and is decorated with Vandyke lace, the points falling upon the upper part of the body. The leg-o'-mutton sleeves, which have each two seams, are trimmed at the wrists with upturned Vandyke lace. A sash having fringed ends encircles the waist and is bowed at the left side of the closing; the skirt and body are joined, excepting for a short distance across the front.

The mode is especially well adapted to combinations, all varieties of woolen dress fabrics uniting effectively with velvet or silk. Cotton fabrics such as lawn, cambric, mull, seersucker, zephyr, etc., will develop stylishly in this way, and all-over embroidery may be united with them for the ornamental sections and facings, while lace or embroidery will form a pretty decoration.

Pattern No. 3155 is suitable for misses from ten to sixteen years of age.

3113
Front View.

3113
Back View.

3155
Front View.

3155
Back View.

MISSES' DRESS.

Figure No. 522 K.   Figure No. 523 K.   Figure No. 524 K.

1890s
Girls' Dress and Guimpe

Figure No. 524 K. — This consists of a girls' dress and guimpe. The dress pattern is No. 3324. The guimpe pattern is No. 2329.

The dress is here pictured made of Surah and velvet and worn over a guimpe of dotted muslin. The guimpe has a full yoke joined to the top of a waist portion that is drawn in to the waist by a shirr-tape. The sleeves are full and are finished with wristbands in which are sewed frills of lace. At the neck is a band trimmed with ribbon and lace.

The body of the dress is quite fanciful in style and has a low V-neck that displays the guimpe, with picturesque effect. It is fitted smoothly by underarm and side-back gores and closed at the back, and to the lower edge is joined a full skirt that is gathered all round at the top and deeply hemmed at the bottom. Upon the front, which is plain and made of lining goods, is arranged a front of velvet that extends below the plain front in two points at the center; upon this is a surplice that is gathered into the arm's-eye and underarm seams, and drawn down as closely as possible at the center under a pretty buckle. The visible portion of the velvet front is decorated with Kursheedt's Standard gold-and-black bands in Grecian design. Broad sash-ties that are plaited into the underarm seams are carried to the back and tied in an immense bow. The short sleeves, which are made on plain linings, fit prettily over the guimpe sleeves and are gathered to stand high and full upon the shoulders. An ornament of velvet which passes beneath each sleeve meets on the upper side at the lower edge and flares sharply toward the arm's-eye, the flaring edges being decorated to correspond with the velvet front.

Dresses of this kind are among the most stylish and becoming modes for little women and will be made up in all sorts of textures. India and China silks combined with velvet will develop beautifully in this way for party and afternoon wear and will be worn over guimpes of lace net or sheer muslin.

The hat is made of sheer muslin and is prettily trimmed with ribbon.

Pattern No. 3324 is appropriate for girls from five to twelve years of age. Guimpe Pattern No. 2329 is suited to girls from two to twelve years of age.

1890
Girls' Dresses

Figure No. 522 K. — Plain and figured India silk and silk mull are here combined in this dress. The body is a round waist with a full yoke upper part and a full lower part both back and front; three tuck-shirrings are made in the top of the lower portions to present the effect of a thick ruche. The full portions are applied upon smooth front and back portions of lining that render the adjustment comfortable and becoming. The fullness of the lower portions is drawn well to the center at the front and back by gathers in the lower edge; the closing is made at the back. The yoke is gathered at the neck and lower edges and finished with a collar, over which falls a frill of white lace. Ribbons starting from beneath the lower portions at each side of the arms'-eyes are carried to the top of the shoulders, where they are tied in coquettish bows. The leg-o'-mutton sleeves are trimmed at the wrists with lace frills that are upturned in cuff fashion. The skirt is full and flowing and its gathered top is joined to the body in a seam covered by a broad, wrinkled sash of Surah that is tied in a full bow at the back. A hem nearly four inches deep finishes the bottom of the skirt.

The mode is especially well suited to wash silks and soft, clinging woolens. It will also make up prettily in wash goods, but for dresses that are to be frequently laundered the waist is rather fanciful. Challis, vailing, cashmere, bunting, serge, *crêpe*, etc., will make up very prettily in this way, either alone or in combination with harmonizing fabrics. Flouncings will frequently be chosen for the skirt.

The hat is a large picturesque shape in straw with a full trimming of ribbon and plumage.

This dress would look attractive on girls from five to twelve years of age.

1890s
Girls' Dress

Figure No. 523 K. — This illustrates a Girls' dress. The pattern, which is No. 3305 is in eight sizes for girls from five to twelve years of age.

Navy blue summer flannel is here pictured in the dress, and white Hercules braid trims it stylishly. The skirt is gathered at the top and joined to the lower edge of the body, which is in a fanciful style and made up over a plain lining. The front is laid in box-plaits from the neck to graduated distances below, the plaits being overlaid with braid that is pointed at the lower ends. The lower edge of the front is gathered and sewed to the lining under a broad belt, over which it droops picturesquely, the belt being covered with white braid. The upper part of the back is a yoke that is shaped in Vandykes at the lower edge, this edge being stitched flatly over the top of the lower portion. In the lower portion are made box-plaits that fall out of their folds a little above the waistline, and the lower edge of this portion is gathered so that the fullness droops with blouse effect over the top of the skirt. Box-plaits laid in the upper part of each sleeve from the wrist edge nearly to the elbow are trimmed like the plaits in the front and the sleeves, which are arranged upon coat-shaped linings, are gathered at the top to stand high on the shoulders. The collar is overlaid with braid, and three rows of braid encircle the skirt above the hem.

All dress goods, such as serge, flannel, challis, foulard, sateen, Surah, India and China silk, Henrietta, camel's-hair and cashmere, will make up prettily by the mode, and fancy stitching and narrow or wide braid or ribbon will be suitable for trimming.

The hat is of straw, daintily trimmed with ribbon and plumage.

Pattern No. 3305 is designed to be worn by girls from five to twelve years of age.

1890
Girls' Dress

No. 3154. — Plain white lawn, embroidered lawn flouncing and all-over embroidery are associated in this instance, with embroidered edging for trimming. The full, round skirt is gathered at the top and joined to the lower edge of the waist, from which it hangs in graceful folds. The waist is shaped by underarm and shoulder seams. The front is laid in four forward-turning tucks at each side of the center above the bust, the fullness resulting from the tucks being regulated by shirrings at the lower edge and at belt depth above. Upon the front are arranged zouave jacket-fronts that are outlined at their curved edges with narrow embroidered edging. The back has a deep, square yoke upper part, and a full lower part that is gathered at the top and bottom and joined to the yoke, a row of edging being inserted in the seam. A narrow belt is applied to the lower part of the waist on the under side and a fancy girdle that is painted at the top and bottom at the center of the front and has the effect of a broad, straight belt at the back encircles the body, its edges being followed with edging. The body and girdle are closed invisibly at the back with buttons and buttonholes. The full sleeves are drawn by gathers at the top and bottom, and a deep, fitted cuff finished at the wrist with a frill of edging is joined to the lower edge of each. At the neck is a standing collar outlined at its upper edge with a frill of edging.

3154
Front View.

3154
Back View.

All seasonable dress fabrics may be selected for dresses of this kind, and combinations of muslin, batiste, nainsook, chambray, etc., with all-over embroidery are particularly well adapted to the style. Merino, camelette, nun's-vailing and similar textures in delicate shades will make up attractively in this way with velvet or Surah of a contrasting color; and lace edging, fancy stitching, braid, ribbon, etc., will make tasteful and appropriate trimmings.

This dress is suitable for girls from five to twelve years of age.

1890
Girls' Costume

No. 3152. — Scotch plaid, red Surah and black velvet are the materials associated in the present instance, and gilt soutache braid supplies the decoration. The full, round skirt is formed of joined straight breadths and finished at the bottom with a deep hem; it is gathered at the top to hang in natural folds from a blouse that is made over a lining fitted by underarm and side-back gores and a curving center seam and closed with buttons and buttonholes at the center of the front. The back and fronts of the blouse are united by underarm and shoulder seams, and the fronts are closed under a narrow box-plait made at the front edge of the right front. Gathers at each side of the closing regulate the fullness at the neck, and the lower edge is drawn by gathers and joined to the lower edge of the lining, the extra length drooping below in characteristic blouse fashion. The fullness of the shirt sleeves is regulated in the customary manner by gathers at the top and bottom, and a round cuff of velvet, ornamented with gilt soutache applied in a simple scroll design between double lines at the edges, completes each sleeve at the wrist. The standing collar is decorated at the top with two straight lines of braid above a scroll design, the decoration being continued along the ends. The jaunty Figaro jacket, which is shaped by underarm and shoulder seams and worn over the blouse, is of uniform depth, and its fronts flare widely from the neck. The loose edges of the jacket are trimmed with braid arranged as on the collar of the blouse, and the short sleeves are trimmed to correspond; the ends of the sleeves meet at the shoulder seams and round away gracefully below, with the effect of fancy caps over the shirt sleeves.

The costume will make up most effectively in contrasting textures and colors, but two shades of camel's-hair, cashmere, serge, merino or other woolens will also develop prettily in this way, with fancy stitching, ribbons, cords, gimps, embroidery, lace edgings or any preferred garnitures in keeping with the choice of materials, for decoration. A pretty development of the mode, intended for party wear, unites while China silk and old-rose velvet. The jacket and short sleeves are of velvet, and a row of Vandyke lace is upturned from the edge of the skirt.

Pattern No. 3152 is for girls from five to twelve years of age.

3152
Front View.

3325
Front View.

LITTLE GIRLS' DRESS.

3325
Back View.

3152
Back View.

GIRLS' COSTUME.

1890
Girls' Dress

No. 3325. — The dress is here illustrated made of plaid gingham and white cambric and trimmed with narrow embroidered edging. The waist is shaped by underarm and shoulder seams and closed at the center of the back with buttons and buttonholes. Five narrow box-plaits are laid in the front, over which are arranged fancy jacket-fronts that meet in points at the bust and flare sharply above and below the points to the shoulder and underarm seams; the free edges of the jacket fronts are outlined by a row of embroidered edging, and the shirt sleeves are finished at the wrists with narrow wristbands of edging and are each covered at the top by an ornamental short sleeve that is trimmed at its lower edge with a row of edging. A standing collar of edging is at the neck. The full, round skirt is formed of joined straight widths that are deeply hemmed at the bottom and gathered to the waist at the top; wide sash-ties of the cambric plaited at their front ends and sewed over the underarm seams are tied in loops and ends at the center of the back.

The fashion may be adopted for any dress fabrics suitable for little girls' wear. When a soft silken or woolen material is selected, the fanciful effect of the dress may be heightened by making the jacket fronts, sleeve ornaments, etc., of velvet or by decorating these parts with braiding, embroidery, ribbons, etc.; the skirt may be trimmed to correspond with the waist.

Pattern No. 3325 can be worn attractively by girls from one to six years of age.

3110
Front View.

3110
Back View.

LITTLE GIRLS' DRESS.

1890
Girls' Dress

No. 3110. — Dull blue cashmere and China silk are here combined, with velvet ribbon and embroidery for garnitures. The full, round skirt is finished at the bottom with a deep hem surmounted by five rows of narrow velvet ribbon; it is gathered at the top and joined to a fanciful body, from which it hangs in natural folds. The body has smooth fronts and backs of lining that are joined by shoulder and underarm seams and covered nearly to the lower edge by a full front and backs, which are gathered at the neck, shoulder and lower edges. The shoulder and underarm edges of the full portions pass into the seams of the lining, and the lower

edges are sewed to position under a deep girdle composed of front and back sections that pass into the underarm seams and into the joining of the skirt to the body. The upper edge of the girdle is deeply pointed both front and back; it is straight across the lower edge and is closed with buttons and buttonholes over the closing of the body, which is invisibly made at the center of the back. The upper edge of the girdle is followed by three rows of velvet ribbon. Each of the coat-shaped sleeves is encircled at the wrist with five rows of velvet-ribbon and has a soft puff at the top that is narrow on the under side of the arm and is closely drawn by gathers in the upper and lower edges on the upper side, its ends passing into the inside seam of the sleeve. A downward-turning

row of Vandyke embroidery covers the standing collar.

The mode may be developed with the quaint and picturesque effect of a Greenaway gown by underfacing the skirt at the lower edge instead of turning it up for a hem, so that it will reach the instep. Ginghams, chambrays, lawns, percales and many other varieties of silken and woolen fabrics will make up prettily in this way. The sleeves and girdle will frequently be made of all-over embroidery, velvet or other ornamental fabrics in contrast with the remainder of the gown, or these parts may be decorated with fancy stitching, cords, washable braids, edgings, etc.

Pattern No. 3110 can be worn by girls from two to eight years of age.

1890
Girls' Dress

No. 3322. — Embroidered hemstitched flouncing and all-over embroidery are combined in this instance; embroidered edging and ribbon rosettes supply the decoration. The full, round skirt is formed of joined widths of the material and is drawn by gathers at the top and sewed to the body. The center-front of the body is composed of a square yoke of all-over embroidery and a full lower-portion that is gathered at the lower edge and turned under at the top, where the fullness is regulated by two rows of shirrings to form a frill. The center-backs correspond in effect with the center-front and close with buttons and buttonholes, the closing being invisible along the yoke. Side-fronts and side-backs lap slightly upon the center front and backs, to which they are flatly joined; shoulder and underarm seams perfect the adjustment. The full sleeves have each but one seam and are gathered at the top and bottom and a cuff finishes the lower edge of each. The standing collar is trimmed at the upper edge with a frill of embroidered edging, and the overlapping edges of the side-fronts and side-backs are outlined with similar edging. The frill edges of the center-front and center-backs and the lower edges

LITTLE GIRLS' DRESS.

3322
Back View.

3322
Front View.

of the cuffs are also trimmed with edging. A rosette of narrow ribbon is placed near the lower front corner of each side-front.

Embroidered nainsook flouncing or embroidered chambray combined with all-over embroidery for the yokes and side fronts and backs will make pretty dresses for little folks; for more serviceable wear, cambric, percale, gingham, piqué and batiste will develop satisfactorily. Cashmere, Henrietta, foulé and flannel are particularly well adapted to dresses of this description,

and upon them fancy braid, bands, rows of narrow ribbon and braiding may be used for decoration. A specially charming effect may be realized by the use of embroidered China silk showing a cream ground and light-pink sprigs; wide Genoese point lace may form the yokes, and narrower edging to match may trim the side fronts and backs, and the collar and cuffs.

Little girls from six months to five years of age will look charming in this dress.

1890
Girls' Costume

No. 3134. — The costume is here illustrated made of plain suit goods and Surah, with a fancy steel buckle and buttons for garnitures. The full, round skirt, which is formed of joined straight breadths, is deeply hemmed at the lower edge, gathered at the upper edge and seamed to the waist, the seam being finished with a binding. The full fronts of the waist are arranged upon fronts of lining fitted by single bust darts and closed at the center with hooks and eyes. Each full front is laid in two forward-turning plaits at the shoulder edge and in five upward-turning plaits at the back edge, and the fullness is closely drawn by gathers in the front edge for some distance above the waistline; the front edge is turned under for a narrow hem above the gathers, which are covered by a large steel buckle, a fold of Surah being arranged in the buckle to appear as though the fronts were drawn through it. A chemisette disclosed in V shape between the hemmed edges of the full fronts is sewed permanently to the lining, passed into the shoulder seam at the right side and fastened with hooks and loops at the left side; and jacket fronts opening over the full fronts and extending below them vary the lower outline and add much to the

stylish effect of the waist. Underarm and side-back gores and a curving center seam complete the adjustment. The gores extend below the waistline to carry out the jacket effect, and are decorated at the lower edge with three fancy steel buttons; the back terminates at the waistline, a wide silk sash arranged in long loops and ends being tacked upon it. The full sleeves are each shaped by a seam at the inside of the arm and are gathered high at the shoulders. A cuff upturned from the lower edge of each sleeve is widened at the ends, which flare at the seam; the sleeve is extended below the cuff by a fancy puff of Surah gathered at its long edges and arranged upon a smooth lining. A standing collar provides a finish at the neck.

Camel's-hair, cashmere, nun's-vailing and various thin-textured woolens will be selected for making this stylish little costume. Velvet of a darker shade than the dress goods may be used for the collar, chemisette and cuffs, or these parts may be handsomely braided or embroidered or overlaid with fancy galloons. The full fronts, sash and fancy puffs may be of China, India or fancy silk. Combinations of plain and novelty dress goods will also develop attractively by the mode, and a single material may be employed throughout, with tasteful garnitures of velvet or silk ribbons, fancy stitching, braids, etc.

1890 Girls' Dress and Guimpe

No. 3288. — In this instance the dress is pictured made of figured India silk. The full, round skirt is finished at the bottom with a hem. The top is drawn by two rows of gathers and joined to the low-necked body, a cording of the material being included in the joining. The full front and backs of the body are turned under at the upper edge, and a dainty frill is produced by two rows of shirrings made near the top, two rows arranged a little below forming a very effective puff between. The fullness of the full front and backs is drawn well toward the center by two rows of shirrings made in the lower edge of each; these portions are arranged over plain lining-portions that are shaped by single bust darts and shoulder and underarm seams, the closing being made in the back with hooks and eyes. The short sleeves are arranged on plain linings; gathers in the top of each upper sleeve-portion produce the stylish high puff effect illustrated and the lower part is shirred.

No. 2329. — The guimpe is illustrated made of mull. It has a round yoke that is gathered at the neck and lower edges and joined to a lower portion, which is drawn in to the figure at the waistline by a tape inserted in a casing. The shirt sleeves are gathered at the top and finished at each wrist with a wristband, to which a double row of mull ruching is applied. The standing collar is overlaid with similar ruching.

India silks and challies showing floral or geometrical designs in light colors upon a dark background will make up with admirable effect in a dress of this description, and when such fabrics are used the guimpe will be of white mull or plain white India silk. The dress will also develop handsomely in a great variety of seasonable textures such as serge, Henrietta, challis, foulard, chambray, cambric sateen, gingham and any variety of washable or non-washable goods. Feather-stitching or rows of braid, ornaments, bands — (bands) or velvet ribbon may provide the decoration when a plain finish is undesirable.

The straw hat is prettily trimmed with a full bow of satin ribbon and an aigrette.

This dress is for girls from five to twelve years of age while the guimpe is to be worn by girls from two to twelve years old.

3318

3288

GIRLS' DRESS. (TO BE WORN WITH A GUIMPE.)

3288
Front View.

3288
Back View.

Glossary

People interested in dolls, and consequently in styles and fabrics used in fashions of the late 19th and early 20th centuries, frequently are confronted with words not now part of our vocabulary. We have, therefore, included a list of definitions concerning terms relating to old styles and fashions which are encountered in books and fashion magazines of the period 1880-1905 and some sewing terms, as well as names of various fabrics and styles unique to this period. While the list is not inclusive, it should enable the reader to understand most of the references made in texts from *The Delineator* and other magazines.

Many of the fabrics mentioned in this glossary have been in common use for more than a century, and thus are familiar to us in present-day use, providing a source of fabrics which may be used for authentic costuming of antique dolls.

AIGRETTE: a spray of feathers or gems worn on a hat or in the hair.

ALBATROSS: a lightweight woolen fabric in which the plain weave has been varied to produce a crepe effect. It is usually soft, but has more body than challis.

ALPACA (mohair): a shiny, stiff, wiry cloth made of Angora goat hair and with either cotton, wool or silk filling.

APPLIQUE: the process of cutting out designs of contrasting fabrics and embroidering or sewing them onto a garment for decorative purposes.

ARMSEYE: the opening in a bodice or dress top for inserting a sleeve.

BALBRIGGAN: formerly denoted the highest grade of fine knit underwear, but now applied to any kind of underwear made of Egyptian cotton.

BANDEAU: a band or fillet for the hair.

BASQUE: a woman's blouse made with a tight-fitting waist and with or without a short skirt or peplum attached.

BATISTE: a semi-sheer lightweight cotton fabric with a soft silky feel and a silky appearance, distinguished from nainsook by its finer construction and finish.

BENGALINE: a heavy corded silk fabric with a silk warp and a cotton or worsted filling.

BERTHA: a wide collar worn around a neckline, often made of lace, sometimes of matching or contrasting material.

BOBBINET: see NET.

BOMBAZINE: a fine twilled fabric of silk and worsted or cotton, often dyed black and used for mourning.

BRETELLE: suspender-like shaped bands worn over shoulders and attached in back and front to a waistband; often used to help support a skirt, and sometimes applied as trim.

BUCKRAM: a stiff, coarse, inexpensive cotton cloth heavily sized, used for the linings and frames of hats.

CALICO: an inexpensive cotton fabric with a plain weave and usually a printed pattern. It is rather coarse, heavily sized, and has a slightly glazed finish.

CAMBRIC: a closely woven, rather stiff cotton fabric with a slightly glossy surface. It was often used for underwear, corset-covers, combinations, drawers and chemises.

CAPOTE: A long flowing coat or cloak with a hood, sometimes worn by soldiers, or a very long mantle worn by women. This word is also used to describe a separate full hood.

CASHMERE (cassimere): a soft, lightweight, smooth material in a twill weave, made either of wool or with a cotton or silk warp, and usually found in plain colors. It was used for babies' sacques and coats and children's fall and winter dresses. The name is derived from the source of the wool — the undercoat of a Kashmiri goat.

CHALLIS (cotton): a medium weight cotton fabric finished to resemble wool challis. It usually has a printed pattern and is used when an inexpensive fabric is desired.

CHALLIS (wool): a lightweight woolen fabric in a plain weave or with a small printed design. It was used for dresses and kimonos.

CHAMBRAY: a cotton material, always made with a colored warp and a white filling, which produces a grayed effect. It was often used for children's dresses and rompers, women's dresses and other wear.

CHANTILLY LACE: a delicate lace of silk or linen, having a six-sided mesh ground and a scrolled or floral design.

CHATELAINE: an ornamental hook, clasp or brooch worn at a woman's waist having a chain (or ribbon or string) attached for keys, trinkets, purse, watch or sewing needs.

CHEMISETTE: a vest or dickey, generally sleeveless, made of fine cotton and lace or net; used primarily to fill a low neckline.

CHEVOIT: a strong twilled fabric woven with a colored stripe or cheek.

CHINA SILK: a thin plain silk with a slight luster. It is similar to "Japanese" silk and to "Habutai" and all are used for lining or making baby dresses and ladies' waists.

CLOSURE: opening of any garment which makes it possible to put garment on more easily.

COMBINATION: a top combined with drawers to form a one-piece undergarment. Sometimes referred to as chemise-drawers.

COUTIL: a heavy cotton cloth used for making corsets with herringbone weave and sleek smooth appearance.

CRASH: a term loosely applied to any cotton or linen fabric which is constructed from coarse yarns in a plain loose weave. Better qualities were used for suits, separate skirts and toweling.

CRAVAT: a band or scarf worn around the neck.

CREPE DE CHINE: a fine soft crepe fabric.

CREPON: a fabric resembling crepe but firmer in texture.

CRINOLINE: a coarse, medium weight cotton cloth, heavily sized, more closely woven than buckram and not quite so stiff.

CUIR: French word for leather.

CULOTTE: baby drawers (as opposed to our present use of the word).

CUMMERBUND: a broad pleated sash worn on a dress, usually with a dropped waistline.

DAMASSE SILK: a kind of brocaded silk material.

DIMITY: a very fine, sheer cotton fabric recognized by small cords or groups of small cords arranged in stripes or cross-bars. (Cross-bar dimity is called JACONET.)

DIRECTOIRE: a style of dress prevalent at the time of the French directory, characterized by a great extravagance of design imitating Greek and Roman costumes.

DRAP D'ETE: lightweight cottons suitable for summer wear.

DROPPED FLY: a flap on the front of boys' or men's pants popular up to the 1840s when a standard front fly replaced it for general use.

DUST RUFFLE: a ruffle, usually pleated in pleats from 1/4in (.7cm) to 1in (3cm) of tarlatan edged with lace. This was placed under the hem of children's dresses for stiffening under the skirt, or on floor-length dresses around hemline to "pick up the dust," hence the word "dust ruffle." This also served to hold the skirt out and to stiffen it.

DUVETYN: a soft, short napped fabric with a twill weave, made of cotton, wool, rayon or silk.

ENGLISH NET: See NET.

EPAULETTE: a shoulder ornament.

ETAMINE: a light worsted or cotton fabric with an open mesh.

FAILLE: a ribbed silk fabric recognized by its flat cord surface, the heavy filling cords being not so rounded as those in poplin and grosgrain, and inconspicuous. In effect, faille resembles taffeta, having about the same amount of stiffness.

FICHU: a kind of ornamental three-cornered cape, usually of lace, muslin or silk, worn by women as a covering for the shoulders.

FLOCKING: decorative trim on fabrics consisting of tiny dots either woven in or later applied in the manufacturing process.

FLOUNCE: deep gathered or pleated ruffles.

FLUTER: a small (about 8in [20cm] by 8in [20cm] by 10in [25cm]) pressing machine with two hollow parallel bars indented on the outside with longitudinal ridges that meshed when turned with a handle. These were heated by means of iron rods heated on a stove and inserted into the hollow cores of the brass rollers. Fabrics were run slowly between the rollers and pressed into the long narrow pattern or ridges on the rollers.

FOULARD: a lightweight silk made with a plain twill or satin weave. It has a rich luster on the right side and usually comes in a printed pattern, although it can be bought in plain colors. It feels light, firm, supple and slippery.

FRAISE FASHION: A lacy neck ruffle.

GALLOON: a narrow band or braid used as trimming and commonly made of lace, metallic thread embroidery.

GARIBALDI: A shirtwaist worn by women, so-called from its resemblance in shape to the red shirt worn by Italian patriot Garibaldi, often full and held in at the waistline by a belt.

GARNITURE: decorative trim of all kinds.

GAUGING: See PLEATING, CARTRIDGE.

GEORGETTE: a very thin sheer silk with a crepe finish.

GIMP: an ornamental flat braid or round cord used as trimming.

GINGHAM: a medium weight cotton material which comes in stripes, plaid and plain colors. Finer grades have a higher thread count (number of warp and woof threads used in the weaving process).

GODET: a segment of cloth wider at the bottom than at the top and used as an inset to produce fullness or for widening, such as in a skirt. (Also: Gore.)

GOSSAMER: a type of very sheer fabric.

GRENADINE: a cloth of very open texture constructed in the gauze weave; usually made of silk and worsted. It often has fancy stripes of different weaves.

GROS DE LONDRES: a lightweight silk fabric of about the same texture as taffeta, but having narrow cords alternating with wider ones. The cords are flat and not so apparent as in a poplin or grosgrain. Often the warp and filling are of different colors, giving a changeable effect.

GROSGRAIN: an all-silk fabric with cords that are uniform in size, especially found in ribbon.

GUIMPE: a blouse with either long or short sleeves worn under open-neck dresses.

GUIPURE: a heavy lace with a large pattern.

HABUTAI (wash or tub silk): a lightweight Japanese silk very closely constructed in a plain weave. It has more body, is firmer, heavier and duller than China silk.

HENRIETTA: a fine woolen cloth.

JACONET: (See DIMITY.)

KILT: a small boy's skirted garment sometimes worn over short tight or bloused pants . . . or without. Usually worn by boys from two to five years of age. The word also designates a girl's pleated skirt.

KNICKERS: a development from women's straight leg drawers to a type gathered on a band below the knees with a ruffle of embroidered edging. Boys aged five to fourteen also wore "knickers" from around 1910 to the 1930s (no lace, of course!).

LAMBREQUIN: a scarf worn over a hat to protect against rain, wind and sun.

LAWN: a fine, sheer cotton or linen fabric of plain weave which is thinner than cambric.

LEGHORN: a hat or bonnet made from leghorn straw which is cut green, bleached and plaited, grown in Tuscany, Italy.

LININGS: See BUCKRAM, CRINOLINE, TARLATAN. (Innerlinings for dust ruffles and stiffening.)

LINSEY-WOOLSEY: a wool and linen fabric with linen threads forming the warp and cotton or wool forming the woof or filler.

LISLE: a smooth, tightly twisted thread frequently made of long staple cotton.

LISSE: a kind of smooth gauze used for ruching.

MALINE: See NET.

MANTILLA: a woman's light cloak or cape of silk, velvet, lace or the like, or a kind of veil covering the head and falling down upon the shoulders.

MASALIA: a trade name for a very fine underwear material which is heavier and has more body than nainsook.

MERCERIZING: an important preparatory process for cotton fabrics or linen. Mercerizing causes the flat twisted ribbon-like cotton fiber to swell into a round shape and to contract in length. The fiber becomes much more lustrous and the strength is increased by 20 percent (hence the advantage of mercerized thread for hand- and machine-sewing).

MERINO: a soft lightweight fabric made originally of fine wool. ALSO, a type of fine wool and cotton yarn used for knitting underwear and hosiery.

MESSALINE: a soft, lightweight silk fabric having a satin weave.

MILLINERS WIRE: a type of cotton-wrapped wire packaged in rolls, black and white, and in several weights, used in making ladies' hat frames and children's hats and bonnets.

MOIRE: usually a corded silk or silk-and-cotton fabric with a watered effect produced by pressing.

MONTURE: a few flowers bunched and used for decoration.

MOUSQUETAIRE: various garments emulating the style of French dandies of 17th and 18th centuries, such as gloves with long wide gantlets, sweeping broad-brimmed hats with dashing feathers and fully-trimmed sleeves.

MOUSSELINE DE SOIE (SILK MUSLIN): a thin silk-and-cotton fabric with very little body, often having large printed patterns in soft colors.

MULL: one of the sheerest cotton fabrics made, mercerized with no dressing, hence soft; crushes quickly and needs frequent pressing.

MUSLIN: a term applied to any plain-woven fabric of close construction, ranging from the very finest grades of underwear material to the coarsest sheeting.

NAINSOOK: a thin lightweight cotton with a plain weave and little or no dressing; sometimes mercerized; not so thin and sheer as batiste.

NET:

1. BOBBINET: a cotton net, the threads so interwoven that they form octagonal meshes, thus making a thin, transparent but strong fabric.

2. ENGLISH NET: a finely meshed fabric made of cotton; the background fabric of many types of lace.

3. MALINE: a fine silk or cotton hexagonal mesh netting, heavily sized, especially desirable for veilings and scarves.

4. **POINT D'ESPRIT:** a fine cotton net with small square spots at close and regular intervals. It is dainty, durable and almost transparent.

5. **TULLE:** a silk net, very delicate and fragile, used for evening dresses, scarves and trimmings.

NUN'S VAILING: a lightweight wool fabric made with a plain weave in plain colors; similar to wool batiste.

ORGANDY: a sheer, stiff, very lightweight cotton, quite transparent and not durable.

PALETOT: a cloak, usually long, with one or more capes.

PANTALETTE: fancy laced and ruffled legs sewn on a band or elastic and worn from knee to ankle under full skirts.

PASSEMENTERIE: a fancy edging or trimming made of braid, cord, gimp, beading or metallic thread in various combinations.

PEAU DE SOIE: a heavy silk with a fine grainy surface produced by tiny cords, enduring and serviceable.

PELERINE: a full-length cloak or coat, often fur trimmed or fur lined.

PELISSE: a long cloak for outdoor wear, sometimes fur lined.

PERCALE: a cotton fabric with a plain weave, usually recognized by its firm construction, its smooth dull finish and its printed pattern, although it also comes in plain colors.

PERCALINE: a lightweight cotton fabric, usually of one color, with a glossy surface.

PINA CLOTH: a very sheer lustrous cloth with a plain weave made from the fibers of the pineapple. It is strong, durable and attractive, but stiff and unyielding.

PLASTRON: a trimming like a dickey worn on the front of a woman's dress, often of a contrasting fabric narrowing from neck to waist.

PLEATING:

1. **BOX PLEATING:** a system of pleating two edges together, skipping a space and bringing two more folded edges together.

2. **CARTRIDGE PLEATING:** a method of pleating great widths of material to be gathered into a small space as, for example, when dressing a china doll with a tiny waist when you want a bouffant skirt. (Also referred to as Organ Pleating or Gauging.)

3. **KNIFE PLEATING:** ordinary pleats of any size with firmly pressed folds going in the same direction.

4. **UNPRESSED PLEATS:** pleats sewn in at the top but allowed to hang free with no pressing or crease marks.

PLISSE: a plain weave crepe or crinkled fabric which has been specially treated to maintain the crinkled appearance.

POINT D'ESPRIT: See NET.

POLONAISE: dress top hanging below the waist and often draped in back.

PONGEE: a medium weight silk fabric in plain weave distinguished by its irregular threads. It is made of wild silk, and hence not so regular, fine nor beautiful as fabrics made from cultivated silk.

POPLIN: a fine-ribbed material found in silk, wool, cotton, cotton-and-silk, silk-and-wool and wool-and-cotton. Its warp yarns are so fine and numerous as to cover completely the coarser filling yarns, thus producing fine ribs across the cloth.

RAMIE: a cloth similar to linen, made of ramie fiber which is strong, fine and durable.

RIBBON WIRE: a narrow (1/4in [.7cm] to 1/2in [1cm]) stiff fabric with fine wire molded into each edge.

RUCHE OR RUCHING: a narrow band of net, lace or fine thin fabric, set in pleats or gathers, applied to trim a dress, particularly at necklines and wrists.

SATEEN: a heavy mercerized cotton fabric with a sateen weave, attractive and durable but not so beautiful nor so soft as silk.

SATIN: a lustrous silk material in a satin weave. Satin is always made in the satin or a variation of the satin weave, but it may be finished with either a crepe or a plain back.

SCRIM: a cotton fabric made of heavy yarns in an open plain weave, strong, durable, semitransparent, easily laundered.

SHANTUNG: silk similar to pongee; this is more irregular in weave.

SHIFT: another name for chemise.

SLEEVES:

BISHOP SLEEVE: wide, full sleeve gathered at wrists.

COAT SLEEVE: a straight sleeve with a slight curve at the elbow, or often made in two sections as for suits or tailored garments.

PAGODA SLEEVE: bell-shaped sleeve (about seven-eights length) with sheer gathered undersleeve.

UNDERSLEEVE: sheer partial sleeve, usually quite full, worn under pagoda sleeves . . . attached on a band to fit over the elbow; gathered at wrists.

SILK BROADCLOTH: a firm lightweight silk fabric with a dull finish distinguished by its characteristic thick and heavy feel without the slipperiness of many silks.

SURAH: a soft but stout silk with a twill weave, usually with a dull surface although satin surah has a rather high luster.

SWISS (muslin): a fine thin cotton fabric rather loosely woven and having a great deal of stiffening. It differs from lawn in being more sheer, more loosely woven and stiffer.

SWISS (dotted): Swiss muslin with dots of heavier yarn at regular intervals. In good grades the dots are woven in and tied so that they will not wash out.

TABLIER: an apron or apron-like part of a woman's dress.

TAFFETA: a plain closely woven, rather stiff silk fabric with a dull luster. Chiffon taffeta is a more soft and pliable fabric. Many taffetas are heavily weighted and do not stand the test of time. (Many grades of taffeta are available in rayon but are usually unsatisfactory because of a bright sheen; they are too stiff to drape well, and do not wear well. They are not recommended for doll clothes.)

TARLATAN: a very loosely constructed cotton cloth, heavily sized, used most extensively for fancy dress costumes and decorative purposes and for ladies' petticoats and dust ruffles.

TORCHON: a type of lace.

TULLE: See NET.

VANDYKES: V-shaped points which form a decorative edging.

VELOUR: a fabric having a velvet-like surface.

VELVET: a pile fabric with the pile usually cut close. Velvets are usually identified further by the kind of backing that is used, thus there are:

1. **VELVETEEN** with cotton backing and cotton pile.

2. **COTTON-BACKED VELVET**, a cotton backing with silk pile.

3. **SILK-BACKED VELVET** with silk pile and silk backing.

4. **UPHOLSTERY VELVET** with wool, mohair or linen backing.

5. **LYONS VELVET** with a cotton or silk back and with very close and firm backing.

6. **CHIFFON VELVET**, an all-silk velvet so woven that the pile is in very narrow stripes so fine that they are not noticeable unless examined closely.

7. **PANNE VELVET**, a cotton or silk-backed fabric, with pile longer than that of ordinary velvet, pressed to give a smooth, shiny effect.

VICUNA: a fabric made from the fleece of a vicuna (a llama-like animal of the central Andes in South America).

VIGNONE: an all-wool cloth, twilled in neutral colors, originally of Spanish wool.

VOILE: made in cotton, silk and wool, a fabric made of fine, hard-twisted yarns with a plain weave and open mesh.

WARP: threads on a loom used to form the length of the fabric.

WATTEAU: a style of back for a woman's gown in which one or more broad folds are carried from the neck to the floor without being held in at the waist, while the front and sides of the gown are "shaped to the person," providing a sweeping, flowing line in back.

WOOF (also FILLING or WEFT): threads on a loom used to form the width of the fabric.

WORSTED: while woolens and worsteds are both made of wool, there is a difference in the length of the fiber, weave and finish. Woolen yarns have short fibers, tend to be soft and fuzzy. Worsted yarns are longer, tend to be smooth and strong.

ZEPHYR: a fine, lightweight woolen fabric. OR light, fine gingham, thin and silky.

ZIBELINE: a thick lustrous soft fabric of wool and other animal hair such as mohair, having a silky nap.

Child's Victorian Fashion

This "Little Girl's Costume," for a size 23in (58cm) doll adapted by Hazel Ulseth and Helen Shannon from *The Delineator*, May 1890, features a bouffant skirt with wide lace trim topped by a unique bodice tapered to a point at center front and composed of an inset of lace bordered by an overlay pleated at each edge. These pleats may be emphasized by feather-stitching, with a narrow lace mandarin collar finishing the neckline. Sleeves are distinctive with high lace-covered cuffs and tremendous upper fullness. Simple bows of narrow ribbon at each shoulder complete the ensemble.

Added to this is a charming cloak with fullness slightly gathered on a simple yoke. Fur bands edge the yoke of the cape, this trim being featured also on a tight-fitting bonnet.

General Instructions

1. Please read through all of the instructions before beginning to work.
2. Place all underwear to be worn under dress on doll before starting to work so that dress can be fitted properly.
3. Cut pattern pieces other than trim of lightweight unbleached muslin or cotton. Assemble following instructions for dress and sleeves. Fit to assure that this pattern is satisfactory for your doll. (See instructions for basic pattern in *Antique Children's Fashions*, page 68.)
4. Try cutting skirts in particular crosswise of fabric for softer hanging pleats and folds.
5. Please note that most of our patterns are made for ball-jointed bodies. In some cases French bodies are more stocky than those of German make, and in almost all cases the arms of French doll bodies are larger, so do check patterns for sleeves to be sure that the pattern you wish to use fits your doll.

Fabric Requirements

LINING: About 3/4yd (69cm) cotton
DRESS: For size 23in (58cm): 30in (76cm) by 45in (114cm) silk fabric or cotton.
LACE: 3in (8cm) wide lace, about 60in (152cm) and 1/4in (.7cm) lace for neckedge and cuff trim.
LACE: Small amount of lace as required for trim on V-inset.

CUTTING INSTRUCTIONS
DRESS
1. LINING: With very sheer silk, sheer linings are added to maintain control. With heavier fabric, this extra lining is not needed. Of sheer cotton, cut 2 dress bodice front overlays, 2 dress bodice backs, 1 V-shaped inset, and 1 skirt rectangle measuring 12in (31cm) by 45in (114cm).
2. Of heavier cotton, cut 1 dress front bodice, 2 back bodices, 2 undersleeves, and 2 top sleeves. (HINT: When working with sheer fabrics, try cutting the lining piece with complete accuracy, and lay this on wrong side of dress fabric. Lightly baste all around and then cut the dress fabric. This will give you greater control in matching the lining and dress fabric.
3. DRESS FABRIC: Cut 2 dress front bodice overlays, 2 dress back bodices, 1 V-shaped inset, 2 upper sleeves, 2 cuffs, and 1 rectangle for skirt measuring 12in (31cm) by 45in (114cm).
4. Cut 1 bias strip measuring 1¼in (3.2cm) by 18in (46cm).

Assembly Instructions

DRESS
5. LINING: Using sheer cotton lining and dress fabric, lay lining of dress front overlay, V-inset and dress back bodice on corresponding linings (or see HINT above). Baste all around. Repeat for upper sleeves with heavier cotton lining.

Girl's dress featured in *The Delineator*, May 1890.

Girl's dress featured in *The Delineator*, May 1890.

6. Place skirt lining on wrong side of skirt and baste all around.

7. TRIM & COMPLETE DRESS FRONT: Matching center of inset and center front of dress bodice lining with neckedges matching, baste in place on lining. Using all-over lace or strips of fine lace arranged as you wish, baste over V-inset.

8. Using dress front bodice overlays, fold on inner line and pleat to broken line shown on pattern, press LIGHTLY and baste in place. Fold on outer line shown and baste to form the finished edges of these two pieces. Trim along folded lines as desired, using narrow lace, feather-stitching, chains of six-strand (or fewer) embroidery floss. Place right and left dress front overlays on lining, matching armseyes, shoulder, neck edge, side seams and waistline. Baste all around.

9. COMPLETE DRESS BODICE BACKS: Matching left and right backs of linings to corresponding wrong sides of dress fabric, baste all around. Fold at center backs on lines shown and baste.

10. SIDE & SHOULDER SEAMS: With right sides together, match side and shoulder seams, pin and machine-stitch. Press seams open. STAY-STITCH around neckedge. Place all underwear on doll to be worn under dress and try on bodice.

11. FITTING BODICE: Lap at center back and pin. Check for fit of waistline, armseye and neckline. TO INSURE PROPER FIT OF NECKLINE, it may be necessary to pull staystitching slightly and tie threads. Leave bodice on doll.

12. NECK TRIM: DO TRY THIS UNUSUAL METHOD OF ADDING LACE TRIM TO FORM A TINY COLLAR. Using 1/2in (1cm) lace, place around doll's neck, and starting at center back pull gently enough to achieve perfect fit over seam allowance. Pin in place. Remove bodice and hand-stitch lace band in place to staystitching. Turn lace toward inside and continue on the inside, forming a second row of lace which will cover seam allowance. Leave basting stitches at center back (placket) of bodice for the moment.

CORDING

13. Cording for waistline. Sew cording into bias strip. Place corded bias around waistline by setting stitching of cording at seam allowance, cord facing upward, with edges of bias to outside of bodice. Hand-stitch on machine-stitched line of cording to bodice waistline. Fold bias to wrong side of bodice,

leaving corded edge out, and secure edge of bias to bodice lining.

SKIRT

14. Machine-stitch 2 rows of gathering along top edge of skirt (already basted to lining), the first row 1/4in (.7cm) from edge, a second row 1/8in (.3cm) from edge. Mark center front with basting or pins. Pull gathering stitches on UNDERSIDE of skirt to fit bodice waistline. Distribute gathers evenly.

15. Place bodice over gathered edge of skirt, matching center front and center backs (center back of bodice placket opened out to match skirt). Check center front of bodice, which will fall in place about 1/2in (1cm) below the gathered edge of skirt. Pin in place all around. Skirt may now be permanently sewn to bodice by hand-stitching "in-the-ditch" where cording is sewn to bodice. OPTION: Skirt may be cartridge-pleated (See *Costume Cameos I*, page 12, or *Antique Children's Fashions*, page 82.)

16. CENTER BACK: Matching skirt edges at center back skirt sew center back seam to within 3in (8cm) of waistline. Match fold lines of bodice placket and hand-stitch to finish placket of bodice and skirt. Sew hooks and threaded loops to placket to form closure.

17. HEM: As you probably know, dolls are very peculiar people. They do not always stand up straight and therefore, sometimes their dresses do not hang straight. Please put doll on stand carefully and use this "real people" method to insure a straight hemline. Put dress on doll. Hang by placing pins around hemline equally distant from floor. Remove dress, fold at pin-line and baste. Even the hem allowance if necessary (in this case it should be about 2in [5cm] deep) and turn edge 1/4in (.7cm). Hem with blindstitch to skirt lining.

18. SKIRT TRIM: Using lace 3in (8cm) wide, place lower edge 3/4in (2cm) above fold of hem and tack in place. If lace of this width is not available, wider lace can be cut to the correct width, folded at top and applied with blind-stitching. This edge may be covered with decorative stitching such as feather-stitching, a band of very narrow ribbon, fine braid or 1/4in (.7cm) lace.

SLEEVES

19. Hand-stitch lace trim on cuff like that used on skirt, and baste all around. Place sleeve cuff on sleeve lining with lace side down (touching lining) matching lower edge. Sew around as shown, *Illustration 1*, clip, turn and press. Baste upper edge of cuff in place. Add narrow lace ruching to undercuff,

this process being much easier when sleeve is opened out. Sew sleeve side seam, allowing for opening at lower edge. See illustration.

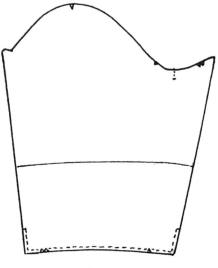

Illustration 1

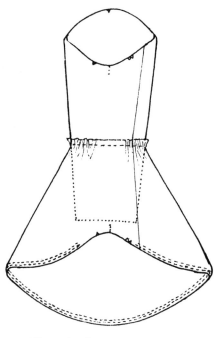

Illustration 2

20. TOP SLEEVE. Sew side seams of top sleeve. Machine-stitch two sets of gathering stitches at upper and lower edges as shown on pattern. See *Illustration 2*.

21. With right sides together, slip top sleeve over undersleeve as illustrated on inset on top sleeve pattern. Make it even with cuff edge. Working with set of LOWER gathering stitches, pin top

sleeve in place and pull gathering stitches to fit sleeve. Distribute gathering stitches evenly and hand-stitch in place. LEAVE TOP DANGLING AT THIS POINT.

22. Put dress on doll. Slip sleeve on doll and work only with undersleeve. Match notches to shoulder seam of bodice and check for good fit. Baste and then machine-stitch undersleeve in place. Repeat for other sleeve.

23. Flip top sleeve up to cover undersleeve. Pull gathering stitches to fit armseye, distributing gathers evenly. Turn under seam allowance along row of stitchng

and pin around armseye. Hand-stitch in place. This method of attaching top sleeve allows sleeve fullness to stand up and puff out fully from seam.

SHOULDER TRIM

24. Loops of narrow ribbon adorn the shoulders. Use ribbon 1in (3cm) by 22in (56cm) for each shoulder as follows: Tie a bow in the center of the 22in (56cm) ribbon, the loops and knot of which should measure 5in (13cm) leaving 4in (10cm) ties at each end of bow. Attach at shoulder seams.

SASH

25. OPTIONAL. Using 2½in (6cm) ribbon

to match shoulder bows, cut 2 lengths 22in (56cm) long, and tack one at each side seam. Tie in back.

The dress is lovely, and it is rather a shame to cover it up, but do go on to the enchanting winter outfit which consists of a full-length cloak (or three-quarter if you prefer), trimmed in fur, the bonnet with a lovely fur halo around the doll's face and a little fur muff to keep her hands warm. We used some scraps of mink for the elegant look seen in the picture, but lovely fake furs are available which will give much the same effect.

Cloak, Bonnet & Muff

CLOAK & BONNET
FABRICS

For these three garments, very soft velvet may be used, lightweight wool, or a fabric which will hang softly. On the assumption that many costumers will want to use velvet, we have included instructions for basting most of the work. This basting is essential when working with velvet because napped fabrics tend to "travel" when sewn together. Also keep in mind that when working with velvet, "steaming" rather than pressing will avoid flattening the nap.

Fake fur may be used for trim, or if you have an old mink collar lying around unused, by all means let your doll wear mink.

Fabric Requirements

CLOAK & BONNET FABRIC. Approximately 36in (91cm) by 36in (91cm) fabric or 30in (76cm) by 45in (114cm)

LININGS: Approximately 16in (41cm) by 45in (114cm) or 18in (46cm) by 36in (91cm) of soft silk or other fabric of your choice.

FUR: About 12in (31cm) of 1in (3cm) banding for bonnet edge, and fur for yoke cut according to template. For MUFF see #21.

CUTTING INSTRUCTIONS

1. Of CLOAK FABRIC cut 1 body of cloak on fold, 2 front and-front-facings, 1 back yoke on fold, and 2 front yokes, 1 bonnet crown and 1 bonnet back.
2. Of LINING, cut 1 body of cloak, 1 back yoke lining and 2 front yoke linings (separate pattern piece), 1 bonnet crown lining, and 1 bonnet back lining.
3. Of FUR cut 1 piece 1in (3cm) by 11½in (29cm) for bonnet, and 1 piece of muslin 3/4in (2cm) by 11½in (29cm). For MUFF see #21.

Assembly Instructions

(Use 1/4in (.7cm) seam allowances throughout.)

CLOAK

4. (Note: Front and front facing are combined in one pattern piece.) Matching notches of front cloak facings to front cloak, baste from top of cloak

Girl's outdoor toilette featured in *The Delineator*, November 1888.

to bottom of cloak, except for area marked by *s, which will remain open to form arm slits. Machine-stitch where basted; then press seams open. Overcast loose seam allowance at area of arm slits.

5. CLOAK & LINING: Fold front facings at center front line and baste loosely at fold (so you will not lose this line). Match lining to inner edge of front facings, right sides together and baste, again leaving the area open between asterisks. Machine-stitch where basted. Press seam allowances open and overcast or blindstitch arm slit seam allowance flat. Lay cloak and lining flat and match seams on each side of cloak. Tack seams loosely from top to beginning of arm slit.

6. COMPLETE ARM SLITS: Matching edges of arm slits, blindstitch together. Since seam allowances have already been turned back, the edges are then completely finished.

7. CLOAK GATHERS: Matching notches at top of cloak and top of cloak lining, baste together. Machine-stitch two rows of gathering stitches on cloak as shown, and put work aside. (If you are using a very heavy fabric, it may be necessary to put gathering stitches in lining and cloak fabric separately, and tack lining gathers over gathers on cloak fabric.)

8. YOKE: Match shoulder seams of back and front yokes, baste and machine-stitch. Press seams open. Repeat for yoke linings. Place edges of front yoke and edges of yoke lining together (double notches) and machine-stitch. With right sides together, match center back and shoulder seams and baste. Machine-stitch around neck edge. Clip at 1/2in (1cm) intervals almost to stitching and turn right side out. (You will note that fabric has folded automatically at center fronts because lining is smaller than yoke, so you now have a yoke lined and finished on three sides.) See *Illustration 1*.

9. (In the first step of attaching yoke be sure to start with the cloak fabric yoke, starting at center fronts. Yoke lining will then be flipped over to cover the cloak yoke.) Match center front line of yoke to center front fold of cloak (where you have already basted in the center front fold), and also match shoulder seams and notches. Pull gathering stitches gently to fit yoke, distribute gathers evenly and baste. Machine-stitch seam. You will note that seam automatically turns upward toward yoke. Smoothing this line with fingers may be all that is necessary on velvet.

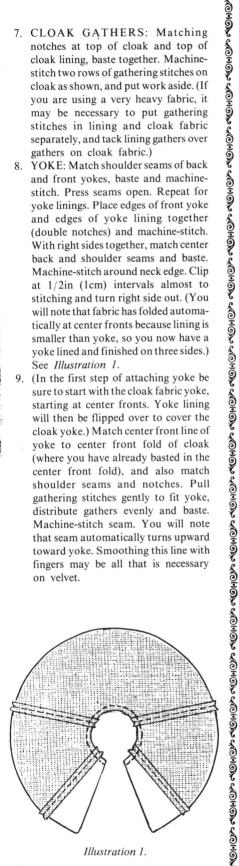

Illustration 1.

10. Turn seam allowance of yoke lining up and press. Lay over gathering stitches to complete lining cloak. Hand-stitch lining in place.

11. CLOSURE: Center fronts of cloak come together but do not overlap. Hand-stitch a hook and threaded loop at neckline. If for some reason the neckline does not fit as you would like, use double thread to run gathering stitches on underside of neckedge and pull gently to fit. This fitting will be almost invisible.

12. HEM: Place cloak on doll over dress and follow procedure for hanging hemline shown for dress, #17. After hem has been completed on cloak fabric, turn lining so that it is about 3/4in (2cm) above hemline, turn and blindstitch in place.

FUR TRIM

13. Cut cloak front yoke trim of fur according to template. Using 1/4in (.7cm) or 1/2in (1cm) twill tape, place on right side of fur and overcast in place all around. Flip tape to wrong side of fur and hand-stitch (or glue). Place fur on yoke, starting from center fronts and work toward center back so possible adjustment may be made more easily at that point. Hand-stitch through twill tape to attach fur trim.

BONNET

14. Match front of bonnet and front of lining, right sides together, baste and machine-stitch. Slide back edge of lining to meet back edge of bonnet crown and machine-stitch the sides (short edges). Turn right sides out and baste long edges (backs) of bonnet and lining together.

15. Machine-stitch 2 rows of gathering stitches on basted line as shown on pattern.

16. Match lower edge of bonnet back and lower edge of lining back, right sides together, and machine-stitch. Leave lining dangle for the moment.

17. With right sides together, match center back of bonnet crown and center of bonnet back, and also match ends. Pull gathering stitches to match bonnet back, distribute gathering evenly, baste and machine-stitch.

18. Turn 1/4in (.7cm) seam allowance on bonnet back lining, flip up and over the machine-stitching of gathers. Pin carefully; then hand-stitch in place.

19. BONNET TRIM. Using fur band and a piece of muslin 3/4in (2cm) by 11½in (29cm), place on right side of fur band. Whip edges together and turn right side out. Finger press muslin. Attach to front edge of bonnet by hand-stitching through muslin. Alternately the twill tape method as described in #13 may be used for fur band.

20. Hand-stitch 10in (25cm) ties at corners of bonnet. Place on doll, tie and **ENJOY THIS VISION OF LOVELINESS.**

MUFF

To complete your doll's outdoor costume, make a muff, perhaps of fur, or perhaps of cloak fabric trimmed with fur. Our instructions are for a FUR MUFF.

21. CUT: Of MUSLIN, a rectangle 5¾in (15cm) by 7in (18cm). CUT: Of FUR, a rectangle 5¼in (13cm) by 7in (18cm). CUT: Of CLOAK FABRIC or a suitable fabric for inside of muff, 1 rectangle 5¾in (15cm) by 7in (18cm), and 2 strips each measuring 1½in (4cm) by 10in (25cm) for ruffles around edges of muff lining.

ASSEMBLY

22. RUFFLES and MUFF LINING. Fold each 10in (25cm) strip lengthwise and press. Machine-stitch 2 rows of gathering stitches along uncut edges.

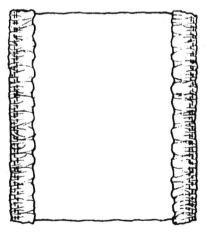

Illustration 2.

Lay along one long side of muslin, matching ends and pin. Pull gathers to fit muslin and pin. Lay the second ruffle on the opposite side, folded edges inside, and pin. (See *Illustration 2.*)

Matching sides, lay fabric rectangle over muslin, re-pin and machine-stitch across ruffle edges. Turn right side out, pulling ruffles outward. Bring cut edges together with muslin on the outside and machine-stitch.

Turn cut ends of ruffles and tack. Divide ends in quarters and mark to facilitate placement of fur later on.

23. FUR. Using 1/4in (.7cm) or 1/2in (1cm) twill tape, place on right side of fur, on long edges of rectangle, and overcast in place. Fold short edges of rectangle together and whip seam shut. (When working with fur or fake fur, a seam like this should be very shallow, less than 1/8in (.3cm), and stitches should be overcast, very close together.) Finished size of muff will be about 5¾in (15cm) by 3½in (9cm).

24. Flip tape to wrong side of fur and hand-stitch (or glue). Mark both ends of fur in quarters to match marks on muff lining. Turn right side out.

25. Insert lining into fur. Match seams and quarter-marks and tack fur to lining.

26. MUFF HAND CORD: Use heavy narrow ribbon or cord about 1/8in (3cm) in diameter and 5in (13cm) long. Hand-stitch ends together and tack to inside of muff on the right side. (NOTE: The seam formed by sewing the fur together should be at back center of muff, so be sure that hand-cord is properly placed with reference to this seam.) For trim you might like to add a band of narrow cord around each end of muff 3/4in (2cm) from edge.

This is a truly stunning outfit which we believe you will find worth the time and effort required. So have fun, and we wish you good luck with your doll costume.

About the Authors

Hazel Ulseth and Helen Shannon have written several doll dressmaking resource books over a number of years. Among their most popular are *Costume Cameos 1* through *5, Antique Children's Fashions 1880-1890, A Handbook for Doll Costumers*, and *Creating Fur Teddy Bears: Mink and Fake Fur. Victorian Fashions Volume I — 1880-1890* is filled with period dresses and suggestions for making them both for adults and children. Ulseth and Shannon have contributed many doll and Teddy Bear costume and making projects to *Doll Reader*® and *Teddy Bear and friends*® magazines. They frequently give workshops on doll costuming and teddy bear making at large toy and doll shows throughout the country.

Hazel Ulseth

Helen Shannon